Talent Acquisition Made Simple: Your Recruiting Guide

Bernard .X Stein

All rights reserved.

Copyright © 2024 Bernard .X Stein

Talent Acquisition Made Simple: Your Recruiting Guide : Streamline Your Hiring Process with Effective Talent Acquisition Strategies

Funny helpful tips:

Maintain a culture of recognition; appreciating efforts boosts morale.

Experiment with different environments; sometimes a change of scenery can enhance focus and absorption.

<u>Life advices:</u>

Nurture mutual trust; it's the bedrock of a lasting bond.

Regularly assess operational efficiency; streamlining processes boosts profitability.

Introduction

This is a comprehensive resource that delves into the essential aspects of talent mapping, offering recruiters valuable insights and strategies for building a competitive advantage in talent acquisition.

The guide starts by defining talent mapping and outlining what it includes, emphasizing its significance in the recruitment process. It highlights several key reasons why talent mapping is important for recruiters, such as building a diverse candidate pool, streamlining the hiring process, gaining competitor intelligence, future-proofing hiring strategies, engaging current employees, and making data-driven decisions.

A crucial section of the guide explores the various resources and tools available for talent mapping. It covers industry trends and social media monitoring, org data, competitor intelligence, financial resources, employee discussion sites, data-sourcing resources, and talent sourcing resources. These resources empower recruiters to gather critical information and insights for effective talent mapping.

The guide provides a step-by-step approach to implementing research into a talent sourcing strategy. Recruiters learn how to use market intelligence and analytics to define job functions and skills needed for each role, personalize outreach messages, modify search terms for hidden-gem candidates, maintain existing talent, and dedicate time to talent mapping efforts. It also offers guidance on presenting talent mapping data to hiring and recruiting managers.

In the final section, the guide explains how to put all the acquired knowledge together and effectively present a talent map. It encourages recruiters to consider future predictions and continually adapt their talent mapping strategies to stay ahead in the competitive recruitment landscape.

This book equips recruiters with the tools and knowledge they need to harness the power of talent mapping and make informed, data-driven decisions in talent acquisition.

Contents

Chapter 1: What is Talent Mapping? 1
    What is included in a talent map? 2
Chapter 2: Why is Talent Mapping Important? 6
    1. Recruiters can build a pool of diverse, qualified candidates 7
    2. Technology streamlines the hiring process 7
    3. Competitor intelligence lets recruiters analyze their strengths and weaknesses .. 7
    4. Recruiters can future-proof their hiring strategy 8
    5. Talent maps can be used to keep current employees engaged 8
    6. All-inclusive talent maps separate high achievers from underperformers 9
    7. Data-driven decisions will result in error-free recruitment 9
Chapter 3: Talent Mapping Resources & Tools 10
    Industry Trends & Social Media Monitoring 10
    Org Data 26
    Competitor Intelligence 33
    Financial Resources 39
    Employee Discussion Sites 40
    Data-Sourcing Resources 50
    Talent Sourcing Resources 74
Chapter 4: Implementing Research into a Talent Sourcing Strategy 84
    1. Use your market intelligence and analytics to define the job functions and skills needed for each role in your company 84
    2. Personalize, perfect, and experiment with your outreach messages 84
    3. Modify and expand your search terms to discover "hidden-gem" candidates 85
    4. Complete progress reports and check-ins to maintain your existing talent 86

5. Continue dedicating ample time for your talentmapping efforts 86
How to present data to hiring managers orrecruiting managers 87
Putting it all together 90
Chapter 5: Presenting your Talent Map 90
Future Predictions 102

Chapter 1: What is Talent Mapping?

Talent mapping means performing research and pulling metrics and other resources to better understand a core demographic when it comes to recruiting talent. Having this data will help you pinpoint and understand the market trends, salary, job titles, and education needed to fulfill your job's requirements.

To do this, recruiters should "map" out a full scope of different data points for each individual role. This will, in turn, help them to better understand the local market and recruit and hire leads more effectively.

What is included in a talent map?

So, what are the key components that a recruiter's talent map should incorporate? Here's a few categories that talent maps dive into.

Websites and Resources

Social recruiting and social research applications can be used to find contact information for key candidates on professional networking sites.

Competitor Company Data
Targeting a competitor's employees can provide a strategic advantage for a recruiter's company by accessing valuable talent, industry knowledge, and
competitive insights.

Competitor companies will answer:
- Industry
- HQ and remote locations
- Talent size
- Regional Salary compensation
- Transferable skills

- Comparable job titles
- Number of job openings
- Team structure
- Regional diversity
- Internal activity: Layoffs, Stock Market,

and Leadership changes etc.

Competitor Social Analysis

This report will give you an idea of how your competitors are presenting themselves online or on social media, such as whether they have a jobs tab on recruitment sites or how they are advertising themselves online.

Heat Maps

Digital heat maps can be created using online search engines and other resources, which enable recruiters to identify where talent is regionally located, as well as where the demand for talent is strongest. Such business intelligence tools provide real-time data to analyze employment trends and gather job posting information.

Diversity Data

Demographic data on candidates, such as gender or ethnicity, can help recruiters find new talent and bring a more diverse workforce to companies.

Skills-Gap Data

As industries rapidly evolve, so do the skills necessary for success. Skill sets for jobs globally have changed by 25% since 2015 (LinkedIn.com) and this number is expected to double by 2027. Yet, we've long relied on insufficient and unequal signals when evaluating talent and predicting success. By using LinkedIn's Skills graph tool, you can make future predictions on needed skills for specific industries.

Candidate Intelligence

Analysts can conduct searches and gather information about candidates, such as demographics data, which makes it easier for recruiters to do their jobs. This will show the number of leads (available on sites like LinkedIn) in specific countries, cities, or states based on data from a variety of sources.

Social Profiles

Recruiters should be able to track all the connections and locations found for individual candidates—whether identified through social sourcing or other recruiting methods.

Search Examples

Every network has users input personal information—where they live, what they do for a living, contact information, interests and more. As such, search tools can be used to link a users' social media accounts—like Facebook and LinkedIn profiles—and provide their email address or phone number in the listing.

Boolean Strings

These are tailored searches through Boolean strings that examine the profiles of everyone in a specific social networking group. If, for example, someone is looking to hire software engineers and wants to know where they live or what their experience level is, they could do some research on LinkedIn by examining all members within their network group.

Public Relations (PR)

This tab contains more information that is useful to recruiters, including news and developments about the company that is hiring.

Candidate Slates

The process of creating a candidate slate involves a recruiter or hiring manager reviewing and evaluating each candidate's qualifications, skills, and experience against the job requirements and criteria. Based on this evaluation, the recruiter then selects a group of candidates who are most likely to be a good fit for the position and presents them as the candidate slate to the hiring team.

You can also include your company's (recruiting metric) ATS data in your talent map, such as:

1. Average hires for specific teams per year
2. Average submittal rates for specific roles
3. Average time to fill
4. Average time to hire
5. Source of hire
6. Sourcing productivity
7. Diversity talent pipeline
8. First-year attrition
9. Quality of hire
10. Hiring manager satisfaction
11. Candidate job satisfaction
12. Cost per hire
13. Offer acceptances rates
14. Employee retention rates

Internal Data Includes:

Past Hire Data:
- Candidate migration
- Education
- Previous company
- Job titles
- Source of hire
- Previous industries
- Exceptions

Offer Accepts
• Where have we successfully recruited from?

Offer Declines
• Where have we had bottlenecks or exhausted our hiring strategies?

• Who are we losing talent to?

Showcase Recruiting Metrics:

A great way to manage the expectations of hiring managers is to show them that you know what the funnel looks like, and it shows them that you are being proactive. The information talent maps can provide extends far beyond what is mentioned in this list and can be further varied
depending on the recruiter's market. For instance, some regions now enable professionals to access government data— something prohibited in other countries.

Regardless of their target location, talent maps remain an effective method to source detailed information on candidates and the market, all of which recruiters need to find those rare high-quality jobseekers.

Chapter 2: Why is Talent Mapping Important?

As a recruiter, you're constantly on the hunt for talent. The best candidates can be hard to find, especially when they're already employed at another company with a stellar reputation and benefits package.

But even with so many factors to juggle in the present, it's still as important as ever to plan ahead—something a talent map is perfect for. From helping you source the best candidates in your field to futureproofing your hiring process, here are the reasons why talent mapping is so important for recruiters.

1. Recruiters can build a pool of diverse, qualified candidates

By building a talent map, recruiters create an extensive pool that includes candidates from various backgrounds, demographics, experiences, and interests. As such, the process of filling positions across a range of skill sets and expertise levels will be far more streamlined, especially when it comes to niche industries or senior-level jobs.

2. Technology streamlines the hiring process

With most recruiters utilizing recruitment CRM software to build their talent pools (we'll review these tools in the next
chapter), they are able to collect data about each candidate's experience, skills, and interests much more effectively. This insight allows recruiters to better match
candidates with open roles, and therefore, increase their chances of filling positions.

As a result, hiring managers can hire more candidates and fill open positions faster, which means that the business is able to find the right talent for any role and move forward with their operations as quickly as possible.

3. Competitor intelligence lets recruiters analyze their strengths and weaknesses

When you know how your competitors are performing through extensive analysis, you can determine where they are strongest or weakest and then tailor your own approach to fill in those gaps.

For example, if one of your competitors is struggling with a high turnover rate in their workforce, it might mean that they have trouble retaining top talent—which could be an opportunity for you! You could offer employees higher wages or benefits packages to try and poach them from other companies before another competitor does so first. Alternatively, you might simply highlight your advantage when connecting to existing jobseekers.

4. Recruiters can future-proof their hiring strategy

Finally, talent mapping is mainly about predicting future needs and building a candidate pool that can satisfy them moving forward. As you develop your own, you'll need to ask yourself: where will this company be in the next five years or decade? What type of employee will they depend on to get to that point? What sort of "talents" should that employee possess?

Depending on your answers, you can then work in reverse, starting at the furthest objective (and the skills, education, and expertise the team needs to achieve it) all the way down to the closest one.

5. Talent maps can be used to keep current employees engaged

Since recruiters will measure a diverse range of candidates when developing their strategy, including those already in the company, talent maps provide an
opportunity for engagement with existing talent.

For instance, if you use the talent map to measure your employees' skills and interests, it may reveal that there are gaps between what they have now and what they want in their careers. If so, you can create a plan for them to help them achieve their goals. This could include training or certifications in new skills as well as opportunities for promotion within the company.

All of this will show current employees that there is room for growth in the company, which can help with retention and recruitment. (You can also use it to show prospective candidates that there is a clear career path within your organization, which could make them more likely to join.)

6. All-inclusive talent maps separate high achievers from underperformers

As you measure the talent within your organization, you'll also be able to see where there are gaps in performance. The data will help you identify the employees who are not living up to their potential and those who could be ready for promotion: Two essential factors that'll give you a head start on predicting which areas in the company could soon have a talent shortage.

7. Data-driven decisions will result in error-free recruitment

According to a study conducted by CareerBuilder: 74 percent of managers and recruiters report having hired an
unqualified candidate for a role, it's clear that, even with so many new strategies and resources, there is more than enough room for error.

Good news: Since talent mapping depends on data-driven recruitment tactics, your decisions will only become more wellinformed and supported by solid evidence the longer you develop your candidate pool. Each time you use a recruitment tool, you'll increase the number of insights, data, and other metrics available to you—which you can later utilize during your talent sourcing efforts.

*** In its simplest form, talent mapping serves as a roadmap for recruiters to follow as a business grows and its needs expand. Still, they aren't set in stone, as talent maps should scale in tandem with the team through frequent updates regarding competitor analysis, resource limitations or expansions, new gaps to fill and more.

Chapter 3: Talent Mapping Resources & Tools

Thanks to the rise of big data, there are now plenty of tools and resources that can help you significantly narrow down your candidate pool. In this chapter, we'll go over some of my favorites—and how you'll use them to craft a full talent market map that helps your organization find top-notch employees.

Industry Trends & Social Media Monitoring

Owler

Owler[1] is a platform that provides insights on business and technology trends. With it, you can find the best candidates for open positions, connect with relevant industry experts to build partnerships, or discover your main competitors. You can follow up to five company prospects for free. Here's a screenshot of Owler's dashboard:

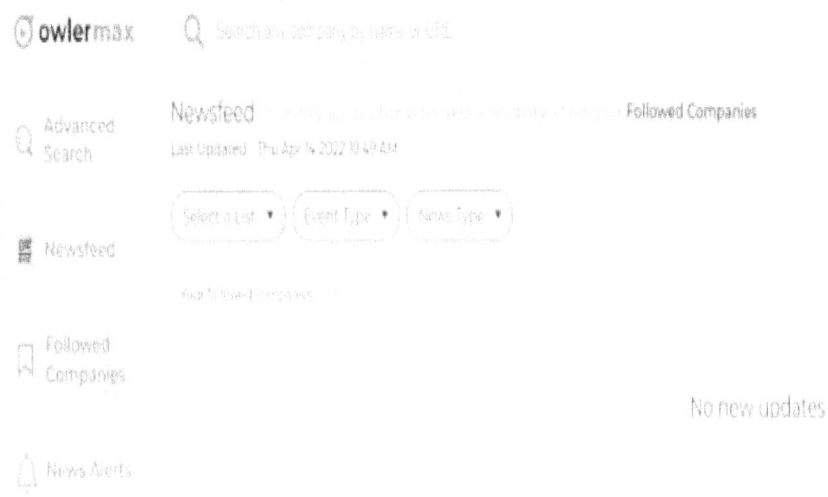

Build custom lists and sync directly into your CRM.
Follow company news and gather

employee data:

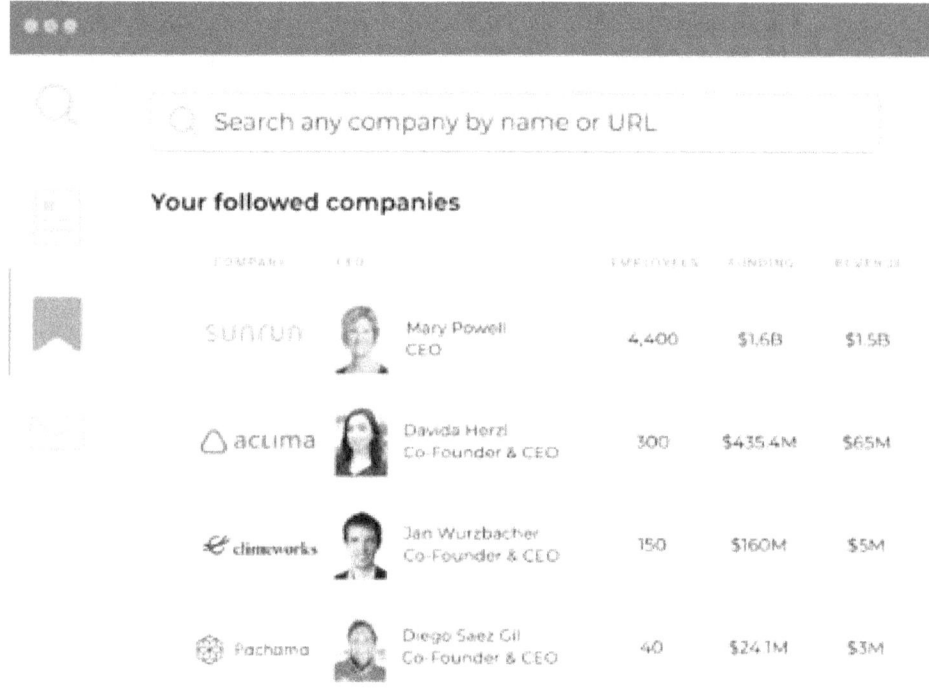

Review market trends in specific industries:

I like how the tool allows you to search specific industries to follow. For example, you can follow updates from Uber's competitors in specific locations.

Integration capabilities include creating tasks to monitor company news.
Connecting Owler into Salesforce, Slack channels, HubSpot, and other CRM tools.

Sprout Social

Sprout Social[2] is a social media
management platform that helps you monitor trends on social media.

You can use it to track mentions of your brand, competitors, and other related keywords in real-time, as well as respond to them directly from the platform. This platform costs about $250 per month to gain access to all of the features.

Sprout's Analytics tools speed up data collection and distribution so brands can focus on the KPIs that matter, inform strategy, and prove ROI.

See all your social media data in one place:

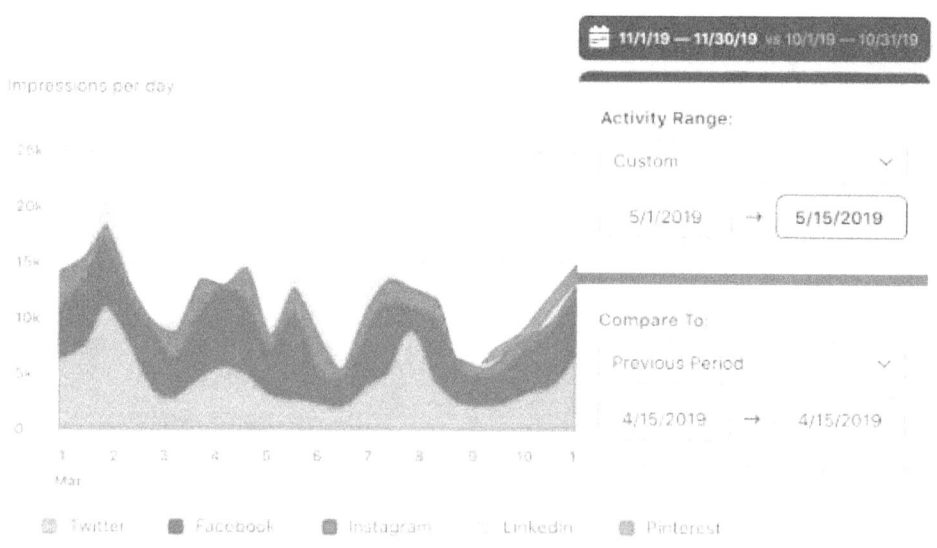

Maintain complete oversight of all
connected social profiles from one location. Save time with a suite of user-friendly, customizable reporting options that scale with your business.

Monitor your competitors:

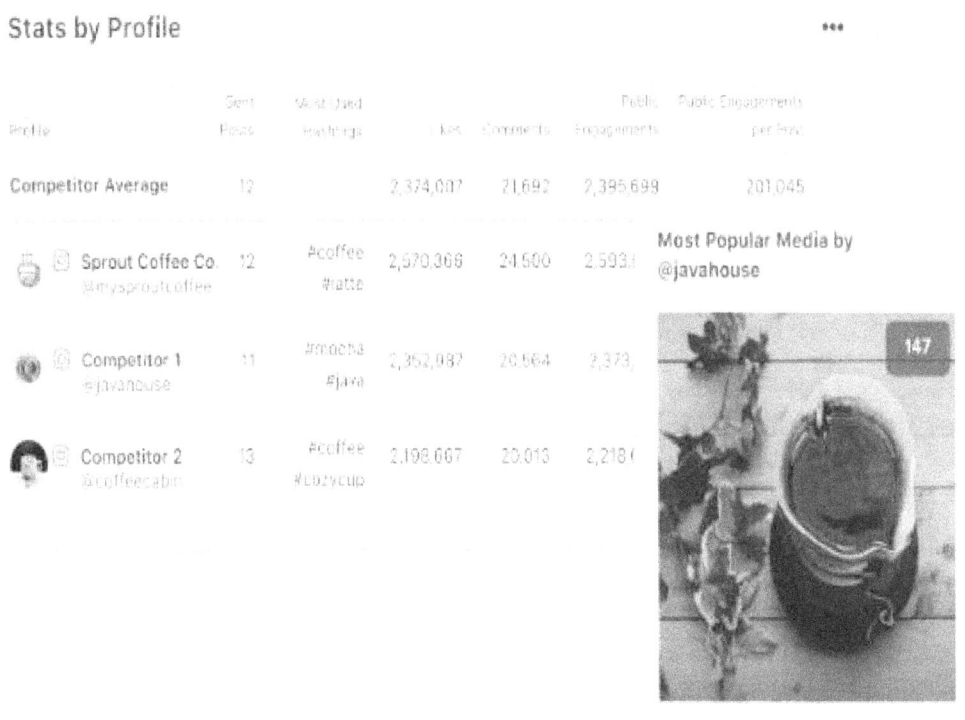

Compare your performance on social to your competitors to find new opportunities. Find and filter historical data quickly to benchmark results.

Identify industry gaps, track share of voice and understand consumer attitudes toward competitors to uncover business opportunities.

StackShare
StackShare[3] is a tool that collects data from company pages, social media, and job boards.

The platform gives companies real-time visibility into all the tech stacks in use across their engineering teams. StackShare Enterprise helps CTOs and other technical leaders make smarter decisions and improve governance

Here's what the search dashboard includes:

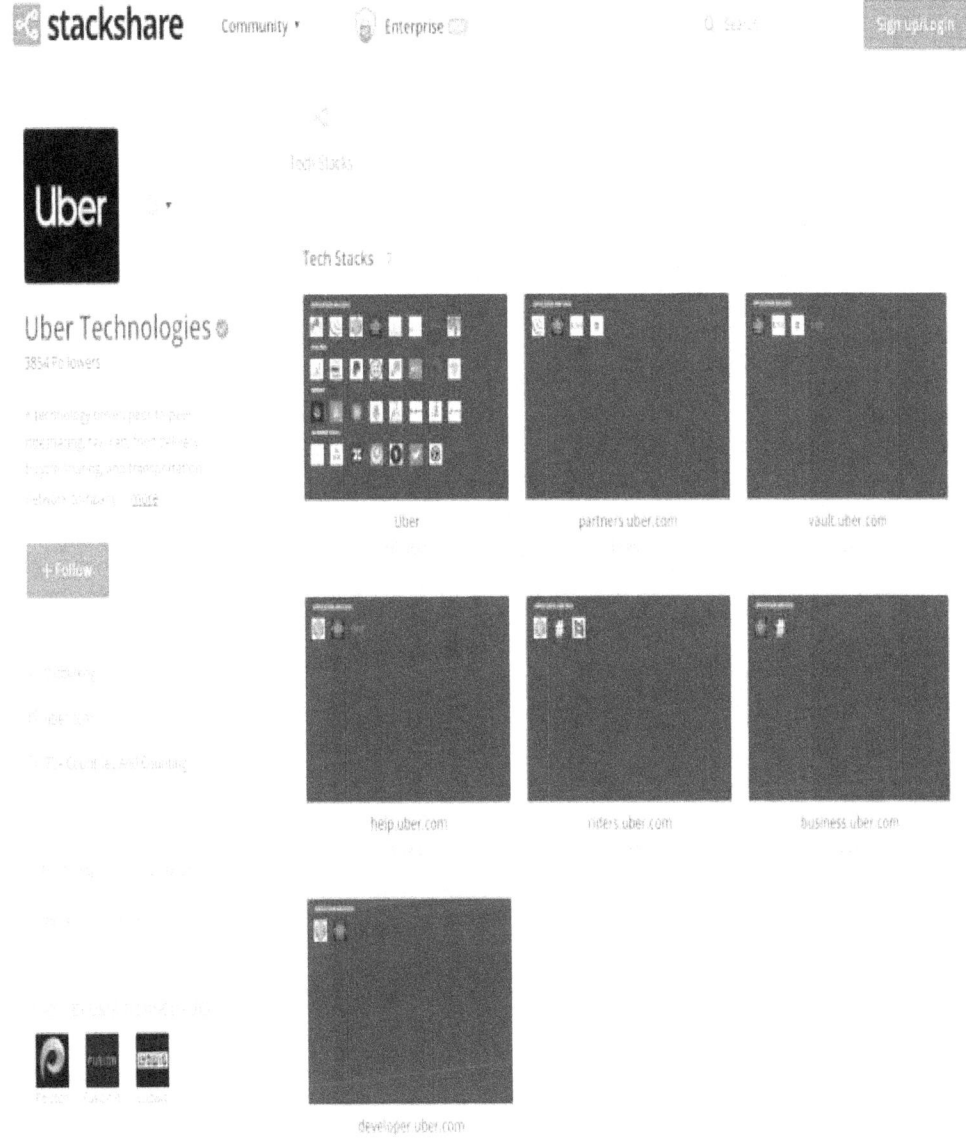

Understand the tech stack of each team's department.

This tool offers a window into the inner workings of most tech-based companies. It's truly valuable intel when searching for potential candidate leads.

Techmap.me

This site[4] helps you find tech companies and startups, tech professionals and tech events in your city. This site helps you find different startups and other tech
competitors in different industries across the globe.

Statista

This is a paid tool, but it's useful for finding the right person for the job. It can help you find trends in your industry by gathering data from all over the web, across 170 industries and 150+ countries.

Search specific industries to learn about current or future trends[5]:

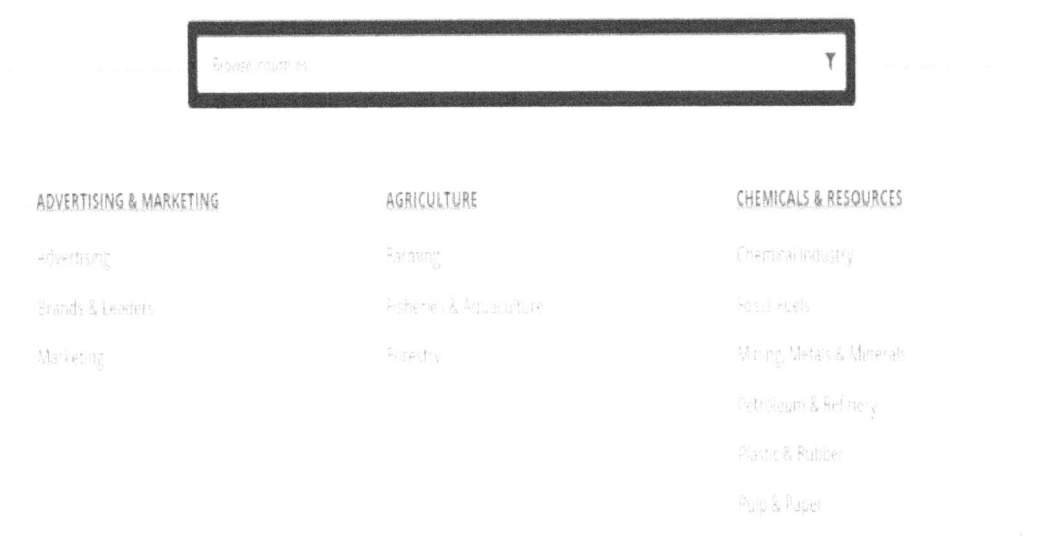

Research industry market trend reports:

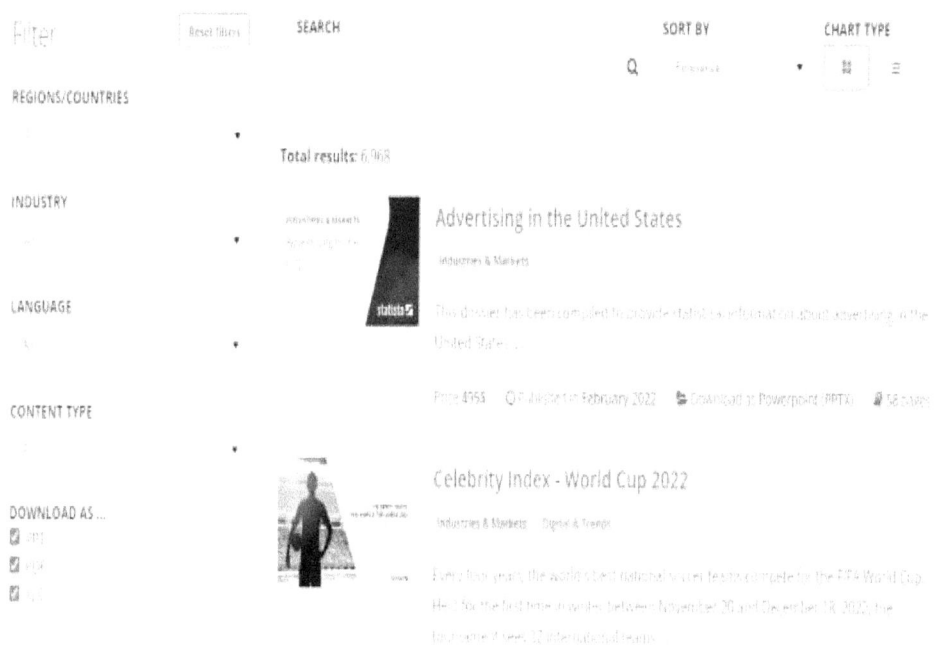

Research specific company reports:

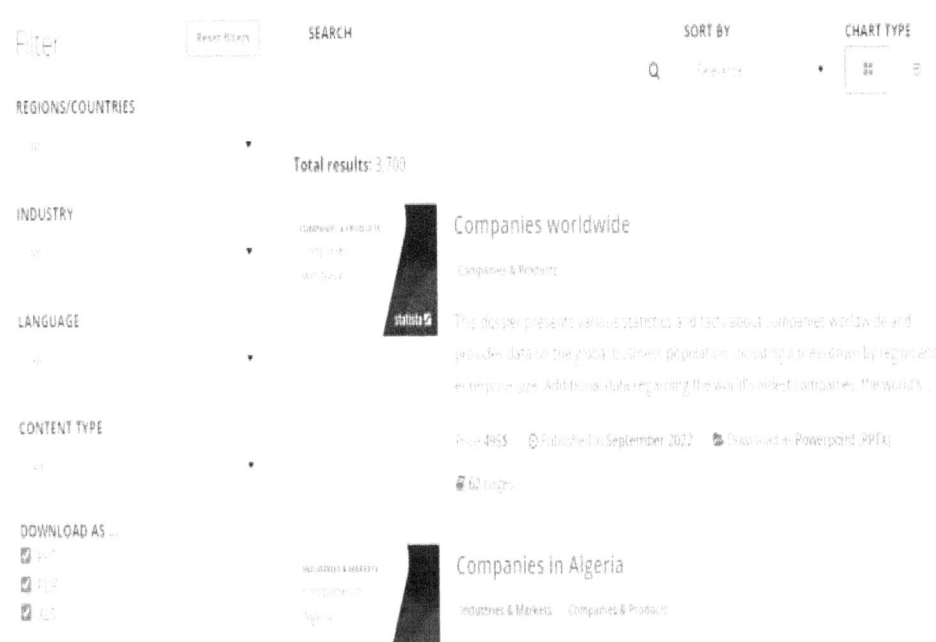

Follow your competition:

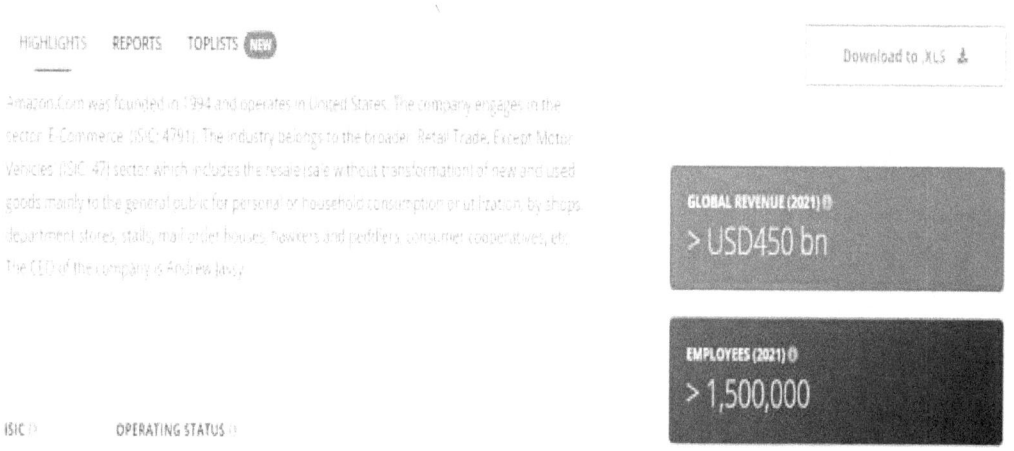

TweetBeaver

You can use this tool to find potential candidates on Twitter, download their account data and timelines, discover their Twitter ID and more. You can also use it to see what they post about work, their interests, and other topics that will help you decide whether they're a good fit for the job[6].

Convert @name to ID	Convert ID number to @name	Check if two accounts follow each other	Download a user's favorites
Search within a user's favorites	Download a user's timeline	Search within a user's timeline	Get a user's account data
Bulk lookup user account data	Download a user's friends list	Download a user's followers list	Find common followers of two accounts
Find common friends of two accounts	Find conversations between two users	Find accounts in a user's followers and friends lists	Find accounts followed by one user that also follow another named user

Welcome to TweetBeaver, home of really useful Twitter tools

Using the tool, you can export a user's Twitter followers into an excel format.

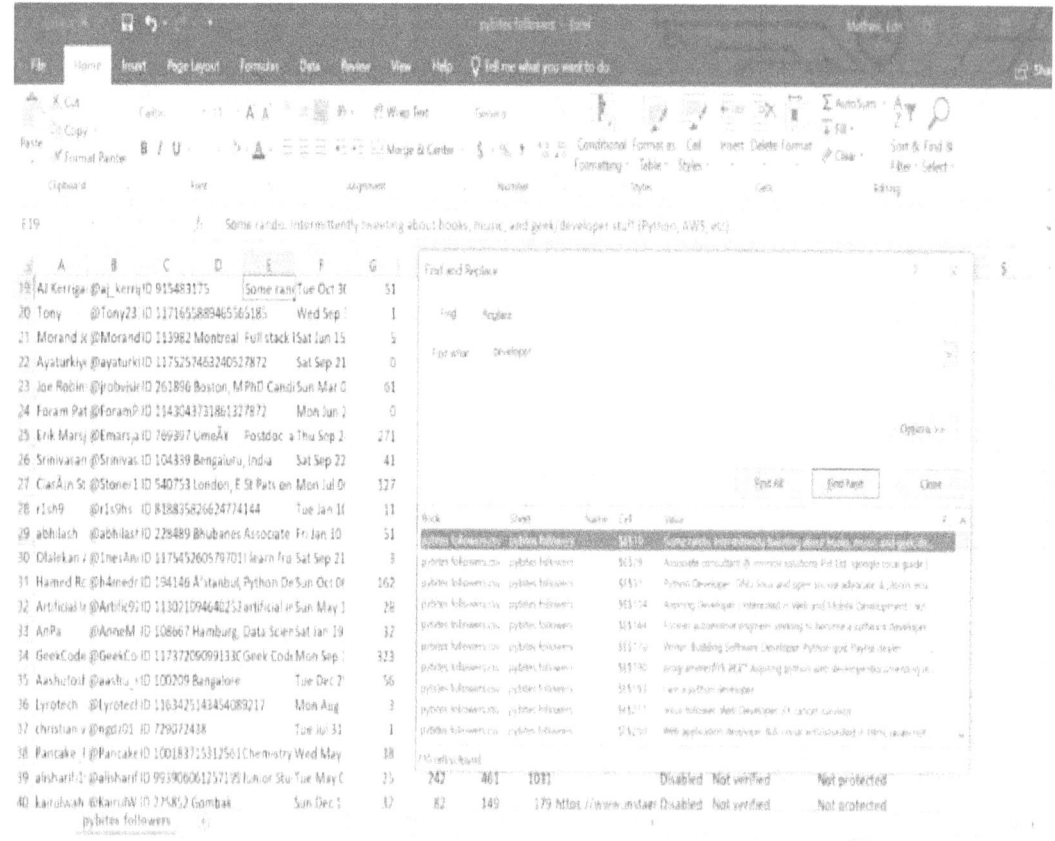

Google Alerts

This notification service (offered by Google), alerts users via email about new results that match the search terms they want to monitor. This includes being notified of the latest web pages, newspaper articles, scientific research, blogs and more.

This will help you automate the search process and help you reach keep tabs on competitors and other company intel.

Simply log into Google Alerts[7] and include a Boolean string. After this, go to advanced features and select the following: at most once a week, web sources, within the United States, and only see the best results.

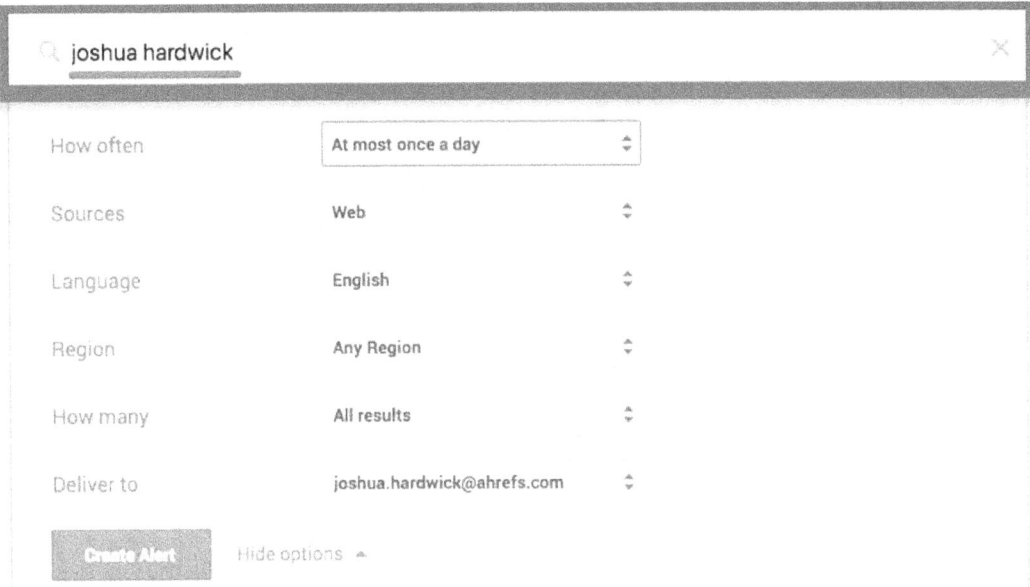

Here are ways to use Google Alerts:

Searching for Active Candidates: Searching for published resumes: (intitle:resume OR inurl:resume) (skill set) ("saint paul" OR 55110")

Searching for companies with layoff news (Select News as the Source)

For example:
layoffs * "Target.com"
("layoffs" OR "downsizing" OR "outsourcing") (company name)

Searching for Client Prospects:
Recently posted job positions based off locations. Search a niche skill set and add a location.

"software developer" ("minneapolis" OR "55111") -templates job jobs

Here's some other search phrases you can use:

("job opening" OR "job listing") ("hiring" OR "now hiring")
("career opportunity" OR "career opportunities")

Finding clients based off niche skill sets: Maybe you've networked with every top java developer in Minneapolis? You can create different alerts to see when a company is actively looking to fill a role. Try using these search phrases and include that niche skill set.

"send an updated resume to" "send a resume to"
"email your resume"
"forward a resume"

Monitoring Competitors

Subscribe to Google jobs. Any time a new job is posted you will receive an alert. You can use this to keep an eye on your competitors' job openings for free.

Org Data

Official Board

Official Board[8] is a free tool to help you find, connect with, and hire the best talent by filtering candidates based on their skills, experience, and education.

This site has a directory of over 900,000+ executives of the compagnies with $100M+ revenue. View over 70,000+ org charts to gain valuable intel on your competitors.

Here's what the directory offers:

Companies:
Learn about your clients' org charts. Understand their industries and their competitors.

Executives:
View the executives' biographies. Contact the executives through our email platform.

Automate Alerts:

Select key words to follow your clients. Receive alerts when executive movements happen.

Track Competitors:
File your clients in folders. Add private notes. Download our data in Excel on your PC.

View current company movements and updates:

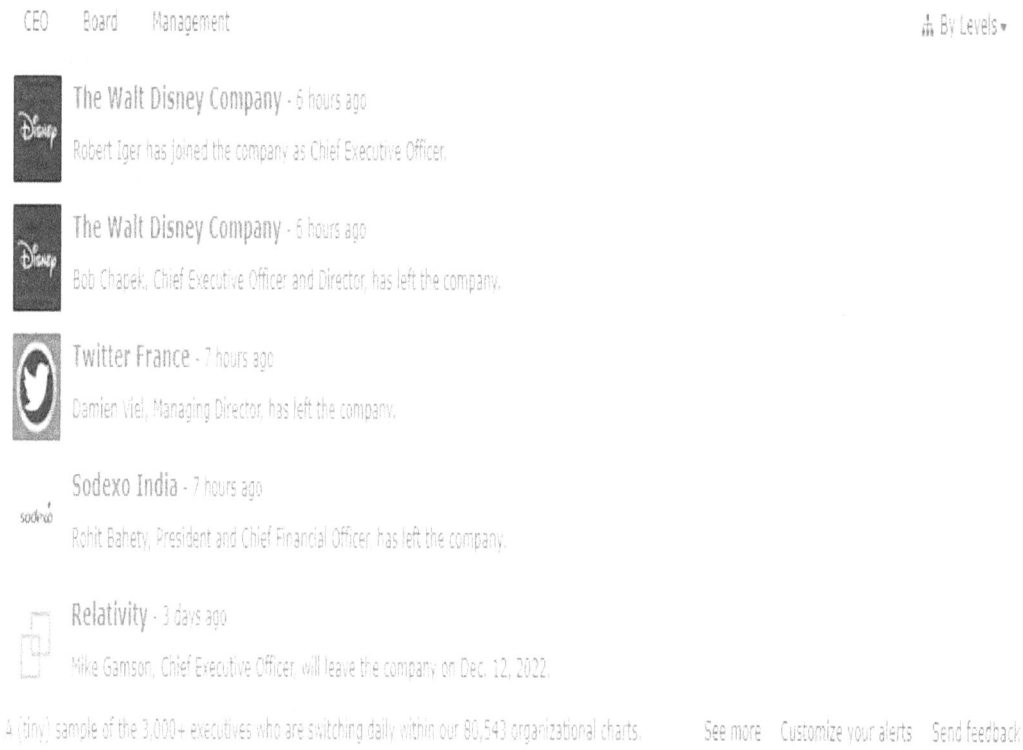

See funding updates on various start-ups:

Funding, IPO and M&A

VC Funding   IPO   M&A

ServiceMax - PTC - 7 hours ago
PTC has announced the acquisition of ServiceMax.

Noatum - Abu Dhabi Ports - 12 hours ago
Abu Dhabi Ports has acquired Noatum.

Total Brain - SonderMind - 3 days ago
SonderMind has announced the acquisition of Total Brain.

Mentoring Minds - Curriculum Associates - 3 days ago
Curriculum Associates has acquired Mentoring Minds.

Expal Systems - Rheinmetall - 4 days ago
Rheinmetall has announced the acquisition of Expal Systems.

A sample of the daily funding, IPO, M&A news within our 80,543 organizational charts.

Wellfound (AngelList)

Wellfound[9] is a platform for startups to raise money, recruit talent, and connect with investors.

The site makes it easy to find new
employees by posting jobs and evaluating candidates based on their skills and experience, job search status, time zone, remote preferences, and completed assessments.

US Bureau of Labor Statistics

The US Bureau of Labor Statistics[10] is a great place to go if you're looking for free data on the skills required by different occupations. They provide information on job duties and tasks, as well as educational requirements and salary ranges.

Their data can be sorted by occupation, industry, geographic region, or
demographic breakdown (gender, age, and race). The site also has a tool that lets you search for job data based on descriptions and locations.

This is by far the best free resource available online to help use for your talent map.

Subject Categories include:
Inflation:
- Consumer Price Index

Pay & Benefits:
- Employment Costs
- Wage Data by Occupation

- Earnings by Demographics
- Benefits
- Compensation Research
- Strikes and Lockouts

Unemployment:
- National Unemployment Rates
- State and Local Unemployment Rates

Employment:
- National Employment Numbers
- Employment Projects
- Job Openings Summary
- Employment Research

Productivity:
- Productivity Research

Geographic Information:
- Midwest
- Southeast
- Mid-Atlantic
- Southwest
- Mountain-Plains
- West

Pull geographic information on individual states:

Datausa.io

Data USA[11] puts public US Government data in your hands. Instead of searching through multiple data sources that are often incomplete and difficult to access, you can simply point to Data USA to answer your questions.

Search States for demographic information:

Competitor Intelligence

Crunchbase

Crunchbase[12] is a database of companies, people, and investors. It has over 100,000 public and private companies from around the world. It also has information on more than 200,000 individuals who have been associated with those companies.

Crunchbase's research tools can help you find new prospects for talent mapping by looking at specific criteria like location (e.g., within a certain radius) or searching a database of employees to find out if they've worked at any other companies, you might be interested in hiring from.

Use Advanced Search and Recommended Companies to filter through companies that match your ideal target profile. Leverage buy signals to identify the prospects in a position to make a deal, push new accounts from Crunchbase to your CRM with our Salesforce integration, and keep tabs on companies with alerts.

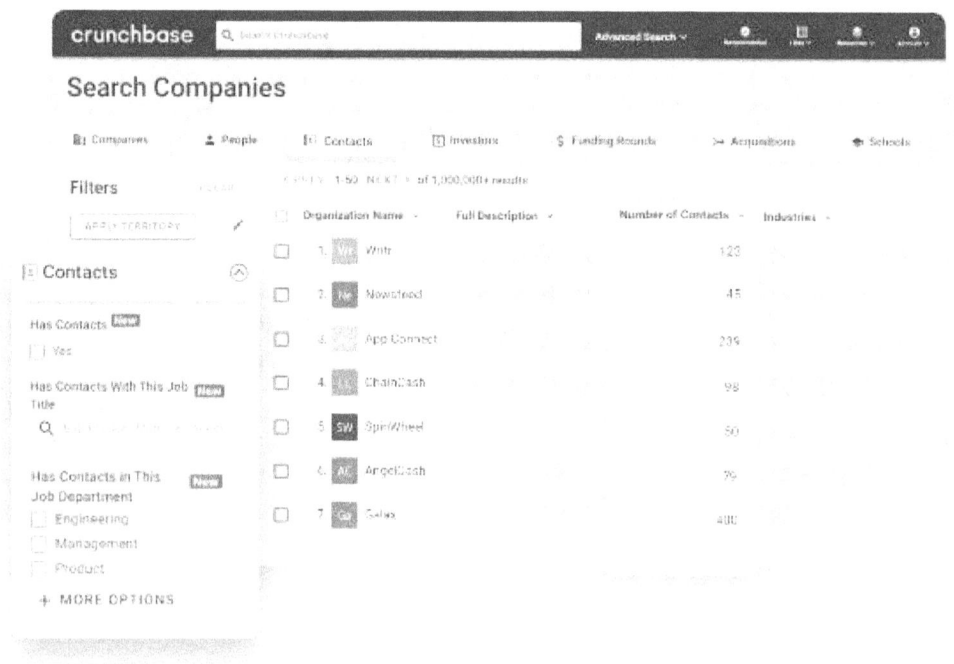

Leverage verified contact data:

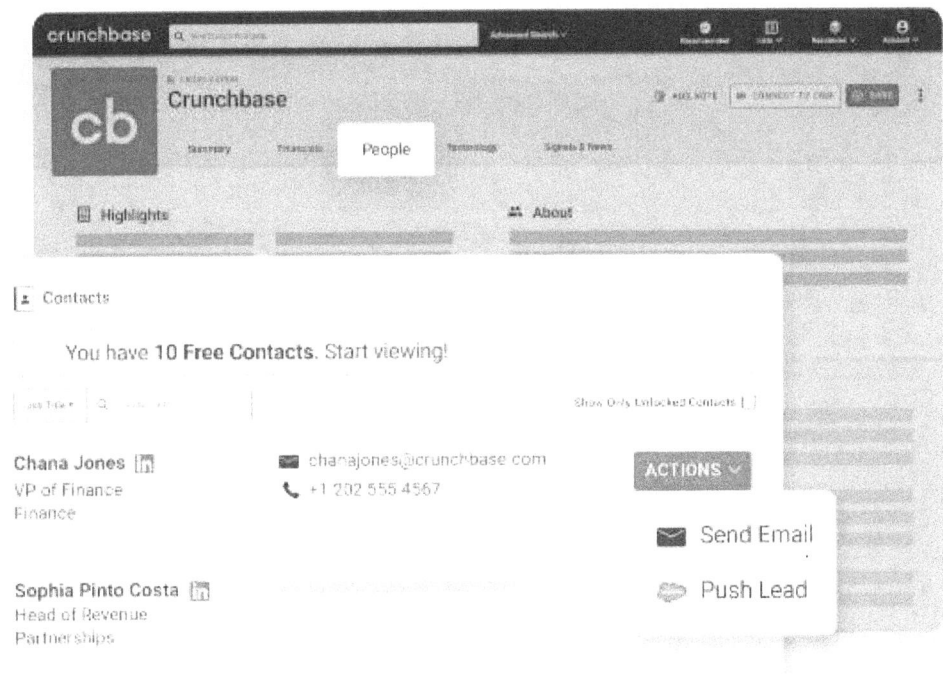

Send intelligent email templates tailored to your prospects or add snippets that integrate Crunchbase insights about them into your own outreach to help you cut through the noise.

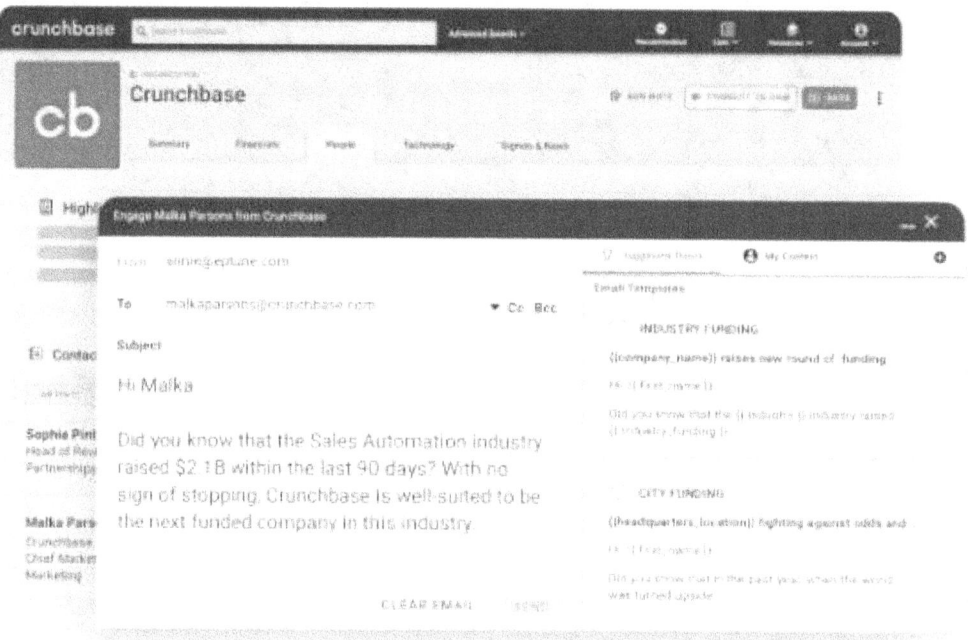

Chartloop

Chartloop[13] is a free and paid tool that allows you to create and share interactive charts, which is a great feature for sharing your data with others, such as hiring managers. Its organizational chart tools allow recruiters to review the active team members of a company including
executives, advisors, and board members. The platform allows you to create org charts that showcase various data points. This would be a great way to showcase org chart data with your hiring manager.
Map the org chart of your competitors or candidates:

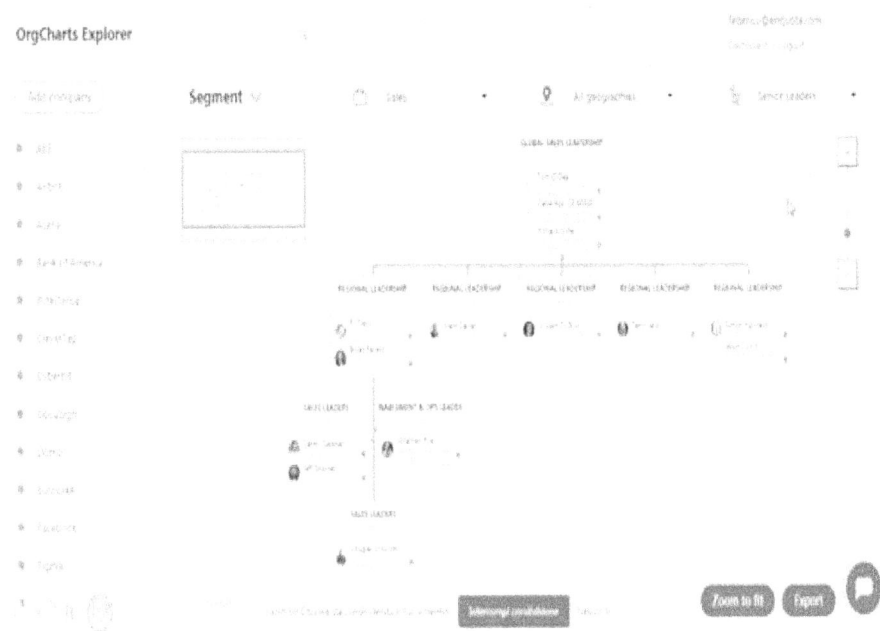

Here's what the platform offers:

• Save long hours of manual research and patching your own organizational charts.
• Zoom in deep into any org from
executive leadership to N-4 resolution.
• Edit hierarchies and add to your target accounts with powerful editorial tools.

"Chartloop is a unique tool that I' ve been waiting for someone to build. In minutes you get a birds-eye view of their team structure and location. This process would take a day to do manually." – Aaron Lintz

EDGAR

EDGAR (Electronic Data Gathering, Analysis, and Retrieval)[14] is a searchable database of SEC filings. It's the official source for public companies to disclose information about themselves, their management teams and corporate governance practices.

Companies are required to file a Form 10-K with the SEC every year that contains eight years of financial statements. If you're looking for information about a specific company's officers or directors along with its financial statements, EDGAR can be an excellent resource for this type of research.

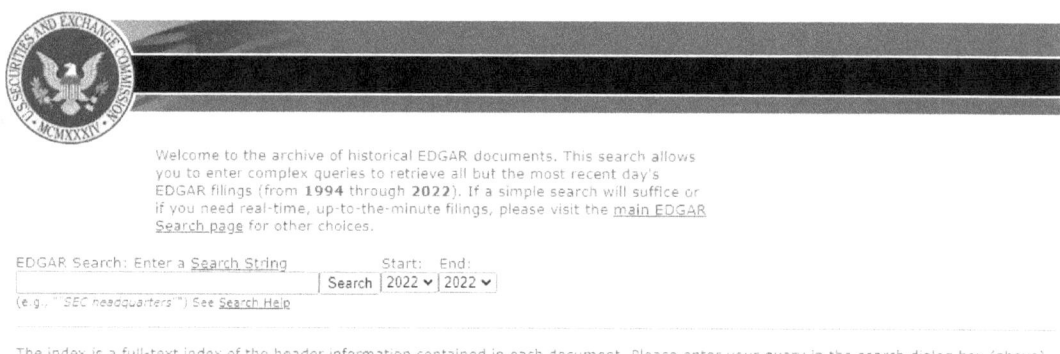

Knoema

Knoema[15] is a business intelligence platform that provides access to market data, forecasts, and analytics, which you can search through to make better recruiting decisions. This is a great tool for understanding more international demographics.

 WORLD DATA ATLAS

United States of America

President: Joe Biden
Vice President: Kamala Harris
Capital city: Washington, D.C.
Languages: English 79.2%, Spanish 12.9%, other Indo-European 3.8%, Asian and Pacific Island 3.3%, other 0.9% (2011 est.) note: data represents the language spoken at home; the US has no official national language, but English has acquired official status in 31 of the 50 states; Hawaiian is an official language in the state of Hawaii
Government
National statistics office

Population, persons: 331,893,745 (2021)
Area, sq km: 9,147,420
GDP per capita, US$: 69,288 (2021)
GDP, billion current US$: 22,996.1 (2021)
GINI index: 41.5 (2019)
Ease of Doing Business rank: 6

Key Indicators
States
Sources
Datasets
Maps
Rankings
Dashboards

ECONOMY
Real GDP growth
GDP
GDP based on PPP
GDP per capita
GDP per capita based on PPP
Inflation rate
Unemployment rate
Current account balance

DEMOGRAPHICS
Population
Population growth rate
Population density
Urban population
Birth rate
Death rate
Fertility rate
Population aged 0-14 years

Financial Resources

IMF

The IMF stands for International Monetary Fund[16], which is an organization that promotes international monetary cooperation and financial stability. It was created in 1944 at the United Nations Monetary and Financial Conference held in Bretton Woods, New Hampshire.

The main purpose of the IMF is to ensure exchange rate stability among its member countries, provide loans to countries with balance of payments problems, make recommendations regarding macroeconomic policies (something businesses certainly need to pay attention to!), and promote effective economic growth.

Research categories include:
- World Economic Outlook
- Global Financial Stability Reports
- Fiscal Monitor
- External Sector Report

Employee Discussion Sites

Fishbowl

Fishbowl[17] is a software company that provides a cloud-based platform for employee engagement, feedback, and culture. Fishbowl's mission is to help companies create the best possible workplace by providing tools and services that enable them to understand their employees better. It now has over 350,000 users across one million groups worldwide.

Follow a variety of categories:
- Company News
- Bowls Communities Discussions

   o Salary Discussions
   o Interview Discussions o Job Discussions
   o Miscellaneous

- Topics Q&A
- Posts
- RSS Blog Updates

Glassdoor

Glassdoor[18] is one of the fastest growing websites used by job seekers. It's like TripAdvisor but for reviews on company work cultures. A large number of job seekers use Glassdoor to find a new workplace. Thus, it has become important for companies to maintain a good rating on this site. Glassdoor is valued at more than one billion dollars currently, which clearly shows how much impact it has been on the job market.

What makes this site unique is that employees can secretly post a review about the company where they are currently working. This gives new job seekers a basic idea about the employer, including the work environment, ability to be promoted, pay, and management styles. Naturally, companies are focusing on increasing their Glassdoor ratings to entice qualified candidates.

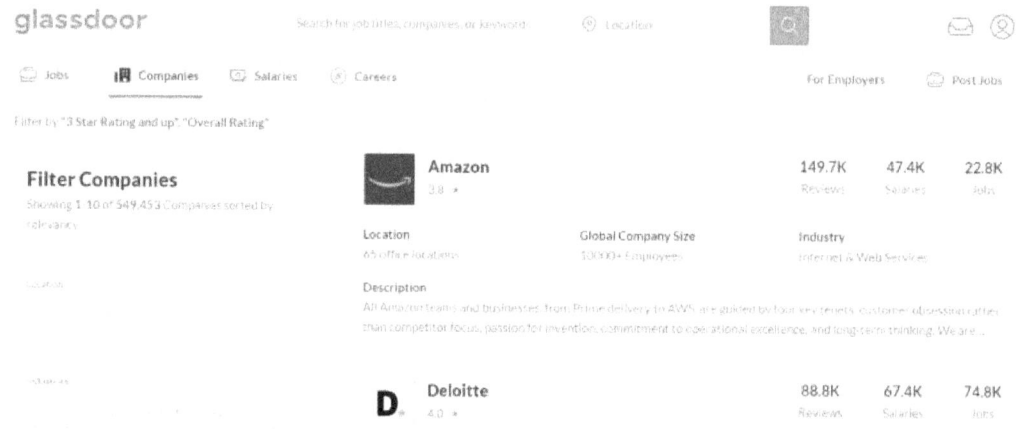

TeamBlind

Blind[19] is another job-search app that allows users to anonymously share their salary, benefits, and work perks with others; they can also connect with others who have the same position or title as them. It has over seven million verified users and over 300,000 companies on its platform.

Categories include:
• Finding Colleges
• Jobs
• Recruiting Talent
• Company Insights

Blind offers an insider view on your competitors' details:

• Internal Transfers
• Company Salary Ranges
• Relocation
• New Grad Information
• Job Hiring News
• Layoff News

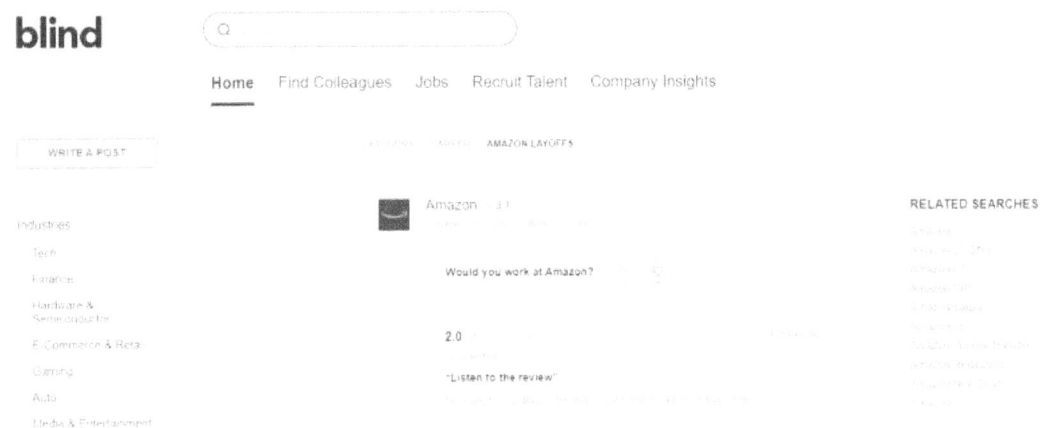

Use this information when you are
conducting talent sourcing searches. Make a list of your companies' competitors and research intel on insider details.

Indeed Hiring Insights

Indeed Hiring Insights[20] is a job search site that also provides salary data, company reviews, and job listings. The site's salary data is based on anonymous salaries shared by people currently working at the
companies with positions listed on Indeed.

This information can be helpful to identify top competitors for the talent you're trying to hire, view similar job listings, and evaluate salary ranges.

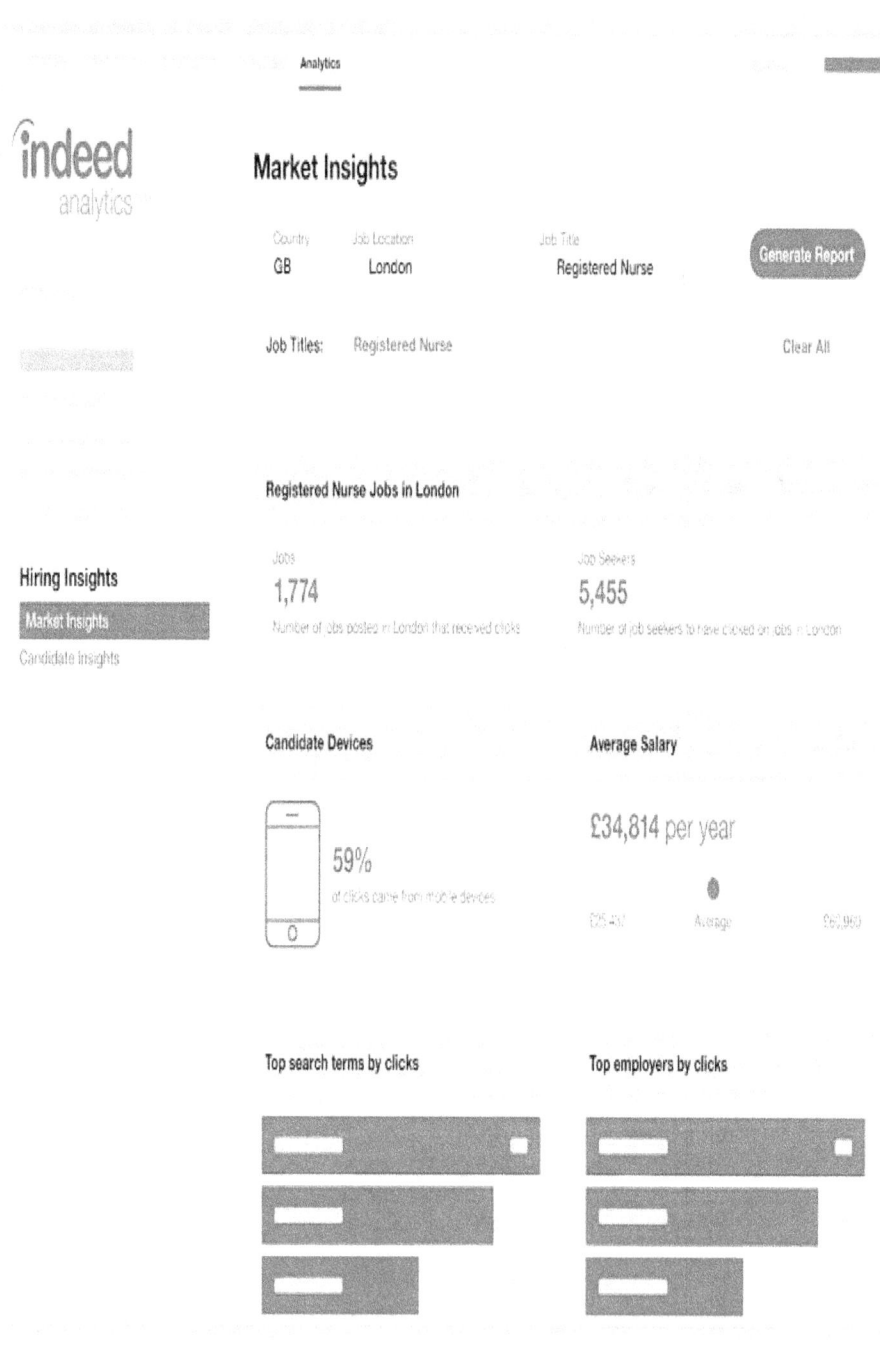

Use this data to optimize your job descriptions.
Data Includes:

- Number of active job seekers in your target market.
- List of your competitors
- Top search terms
- Average number of job applicants
- Other market demographics
- Average industry salary comp ranges

Levels.fyi
Was a site created to help professionals compare career levels across tech companies.

As they started collecting leveling and salary information, we noticed that our data looked very different from what we saw on other sites. Whether intentional or the consequence of the market changing rapidly, published compensation numbers seemed lower than our data. It turns out that salary transparency becomes complicated when data is manipulated, stale, or worst, intentionally suppressed.

The site uses a combination of verified data and leveling information to help employees understand what they should be getting paid.

Here's what you can find on Levels.fyi:

- Search by location
- Search by company and level
- Search by specific job titles

Compare your top competitors:

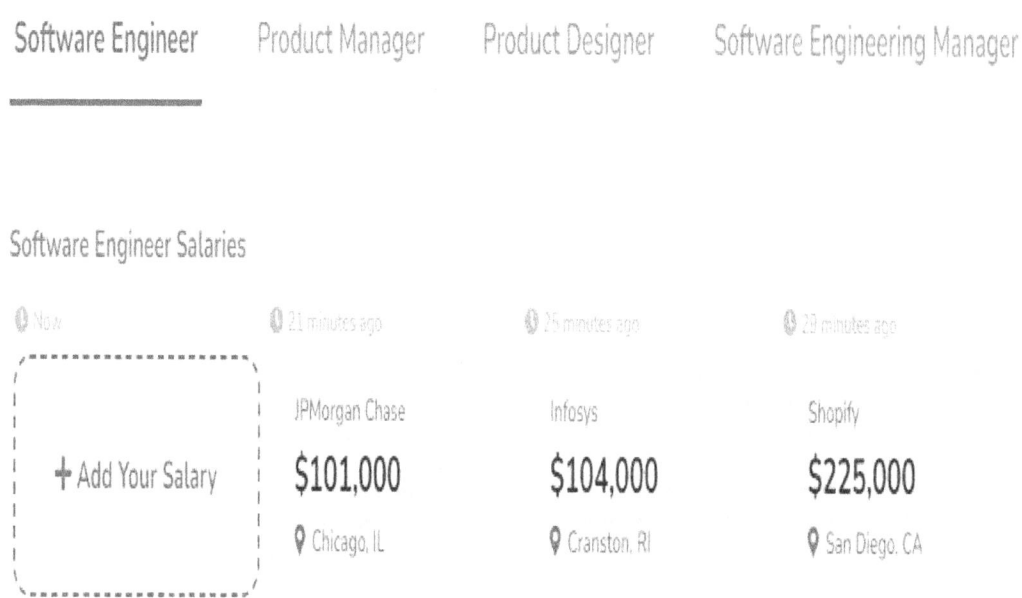

Research company job levels:

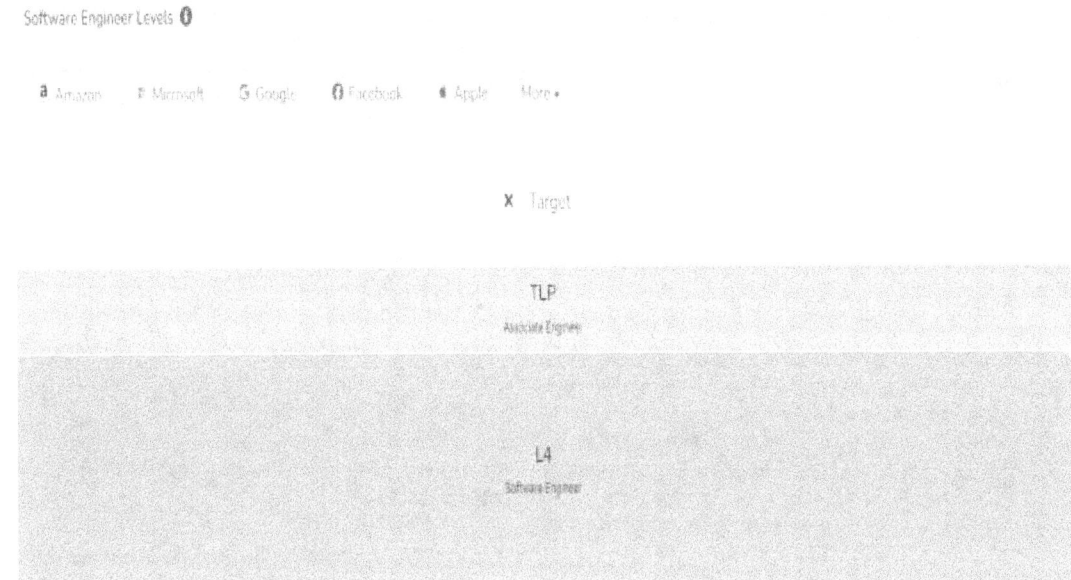

Review specific company intel:

Software Engineer

LEVEL	TAG
Analyst	Full Stack

Average Yearly Total Comp

$101,000

Details

- JPMorgan Chase
- Chicago, IL
- Employee as of 01/11/2023
- Hybrid

Comp Details

Base Salary

STOCK

Average Annual Total Stock (RSUs)

BONUS

Annual Target Bonus

Years at Company	Years of Experience
1 yr	1 yr

TheLayoff.com

Here, users can search through the latest news and rumors about layoffs, or they can post their own personal experiences with being fired from a job on the forums page.

The workforce reduction process is inherently secretive and plagued with rumors. Companies release little or no details while planning such resource actions. On the other hand, the lives of each of us may be greatly impacted by these topsecret decisions—hence all the anxiety that workers may experience.

Enter TheLayoff.com[21]—The purpose of this site is to provide a space for anyone who'd like to discuss the possibility, likelihood or impacts of layoffs in a company of interest.

Data-Sourcing Resources

TalentNeuron

TalentNeuron[22] provides market intelligence technology tools, which are powered by large-scale data analytics. Recruiters can use the resource to receive a clear view of the latest talent market developments for 7,500 companies ranging across 600 cities and 90 global roles. 1. Use a resume to find job leads and data. 2. Search current job postings.
3. Explore employers and job sites. 4. Discover trends in the job market. 5. Explore historic data.
6. Create recurring email alerts.
7. Save and share common searches.

TalentNeuron is a real-time, big data tool that:
• Aggregates information from millions of online job postings.
• Integrates this information with other data sources.
• Presents it in an advanced user interface.

Notable Features
• Robust data sources.
• Current within the past 24 hours.
• Contains extremely flexible search criteria
• Rich with industry occupations and functions.

Dashboard view of TalentNeuron: Start with a versatile "New Search" page. Click "Analyze" after entering search parameters and review the data in the middle and right column.

It then takes you to the "Summary" page . Here, you can explore the information and adjust the results with the filters in the left column. Filters Include: Job Postings:

This page provides a listing of *currently available* job postings that match your search criteria and filters. If you are mainly interested in **job opportunities**, this will be the first page to visit after a search. It may even be where you want to start.

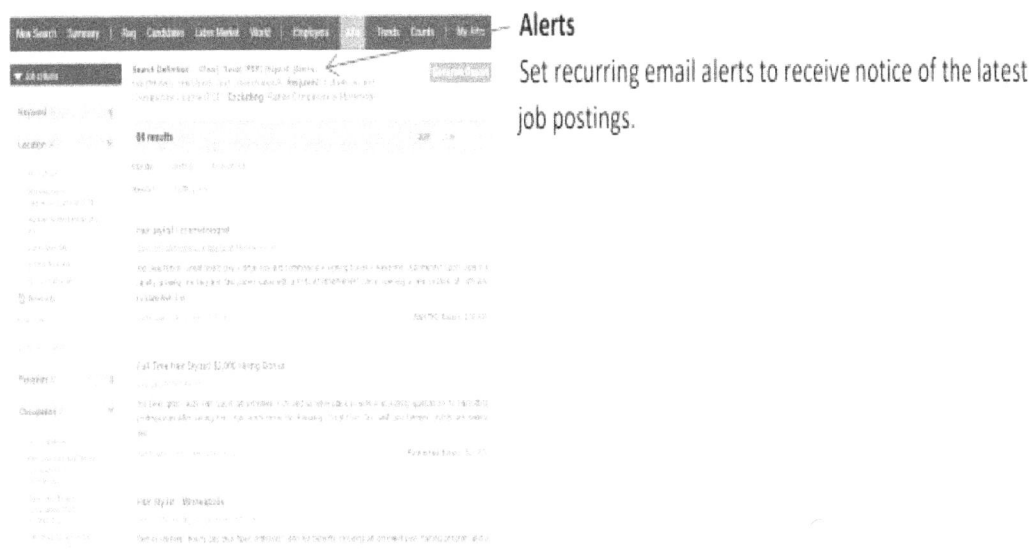

Alerts

Set recurring email alerts to receive notice of the latest job postings.

Employers:

Information available through the Employers tab helps you with close-up views of the *currently available* postings posted by specific companies in your area.

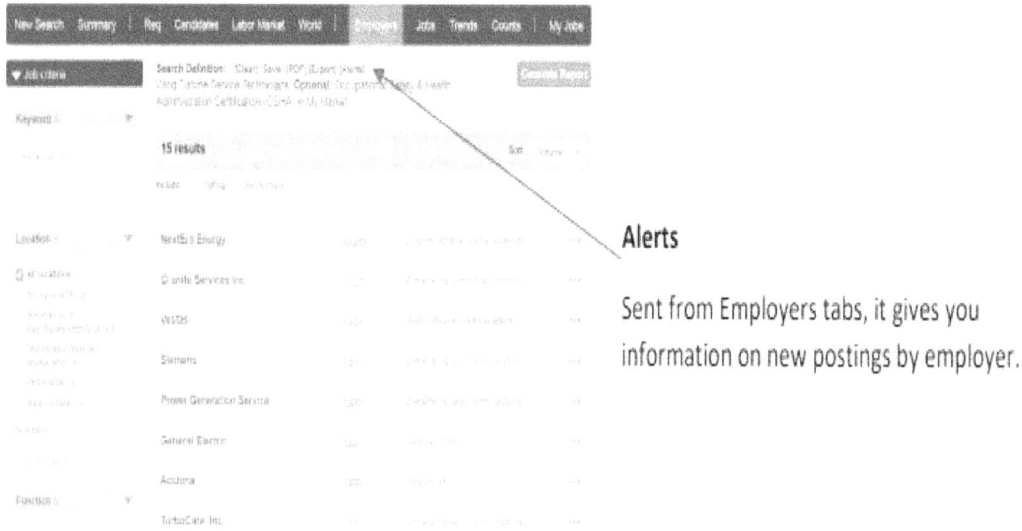

Alerts

Sent from Employers tabs, it gives you information on new postings by employer.

Historic Data:
Labor Market Trends:

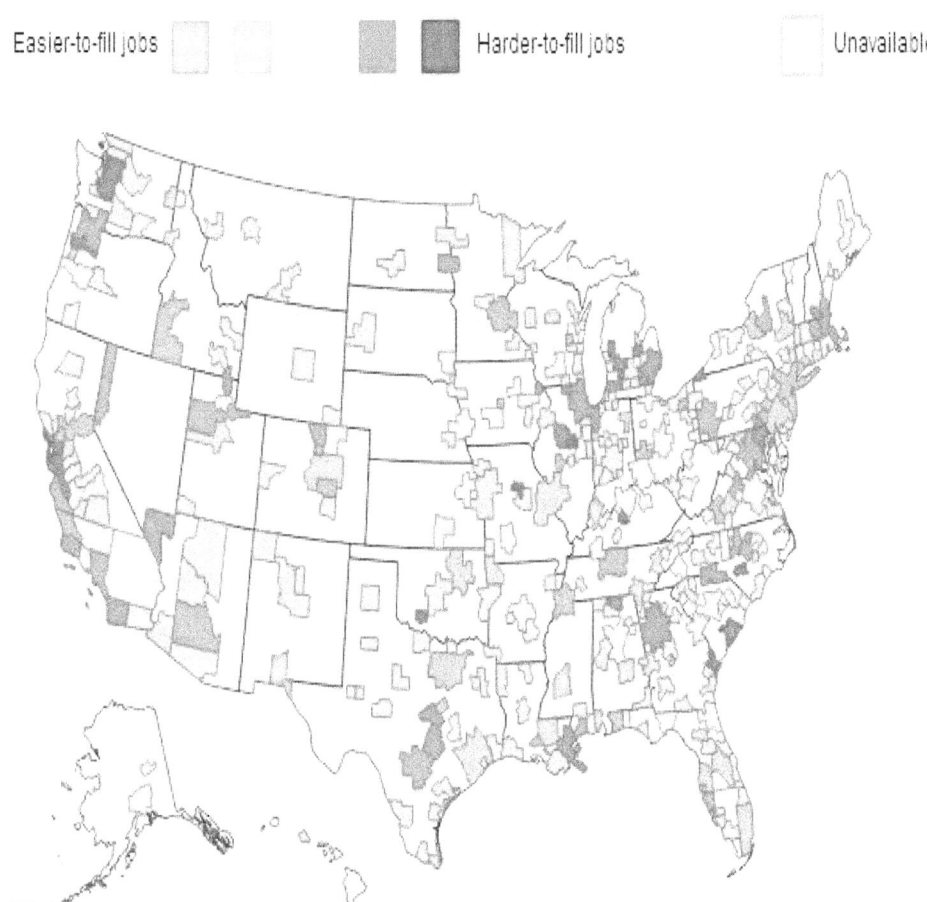

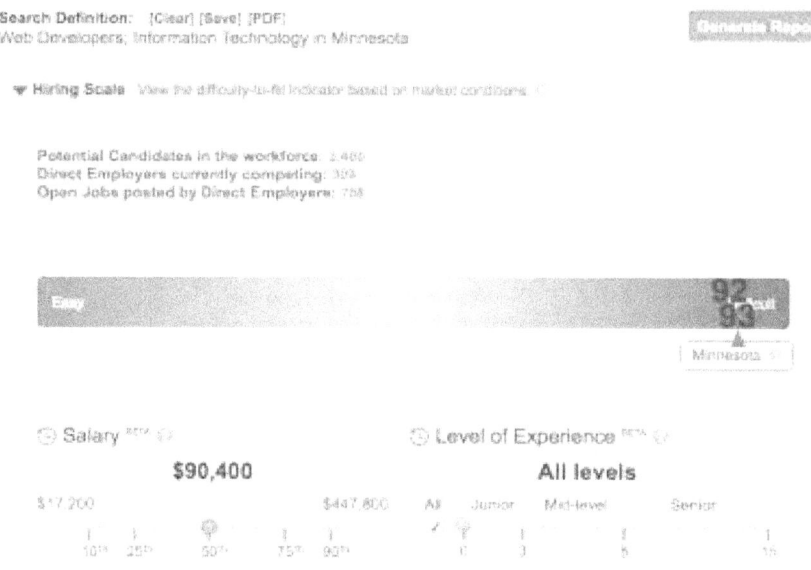

See the average salary ranges per demographic locations.

Candidates:

On this page, you can gather information about the types of people currently in the labor force that have the skills and education necessary to do the job.

You also have access to social media sites to view potential candidates matching your search criteria as well as candidate demographic information.

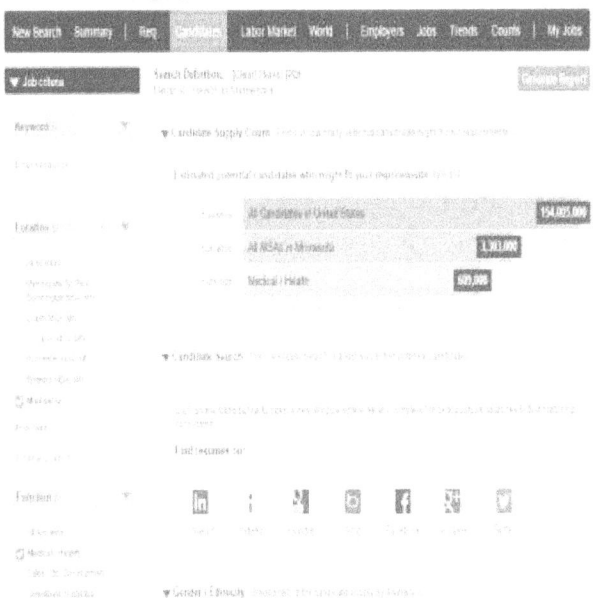

Onet

O*NET OnLine[23] is an application that was created for the general public to provide
broad access to the O*NET database of
occupational information. O*NET OnLine
offers a variety of search options and
occupational data, while My Next Move is a streamlined application for students and
job seekers. Both applications were
developed for the U.S. Department of Labor by the National Center for O*NET
Development.

The O*NET database includes information on skills, abilities, knowledges, work
activities, and interests associated with
occupations. This information can be used to facilitate career exploration, vocational counseling, and a variety of human resource functions, such as developing job orders and position descriptions and aligning training with current workplace needs.

Here's what the site offers Recruiters:

- Develop effective job descriptions quickly and easily.
- Expand the pool of quality candidates for open positions.
- Define employee and/or job-specific success factors.
- Align organizational development with workplace needs.
- Refine recruitment and training goals.
- Design competitive compensation and promotion systems.

WhoKnows

This tool offers a number of products. The one that I would recommend for talent mapping would be the WhoKnows Enterprise[24].

Empower HR initiatives with people analytics and super-charge internal staffing and collaboration.
This alternative option to TalentNeuron offers many of the same services and will help you gain insights into recruiting, assessing, and retaining talent. WhoKnows also advertises a free trial to try out their services.

If you are thinking of potentially using a talent analytics company but aren't sure if it is worth the investment, this may be a perfect option. WhoKnows has a few advantages such as no IT integration needed, which can make it more affordable for companies to begin using.

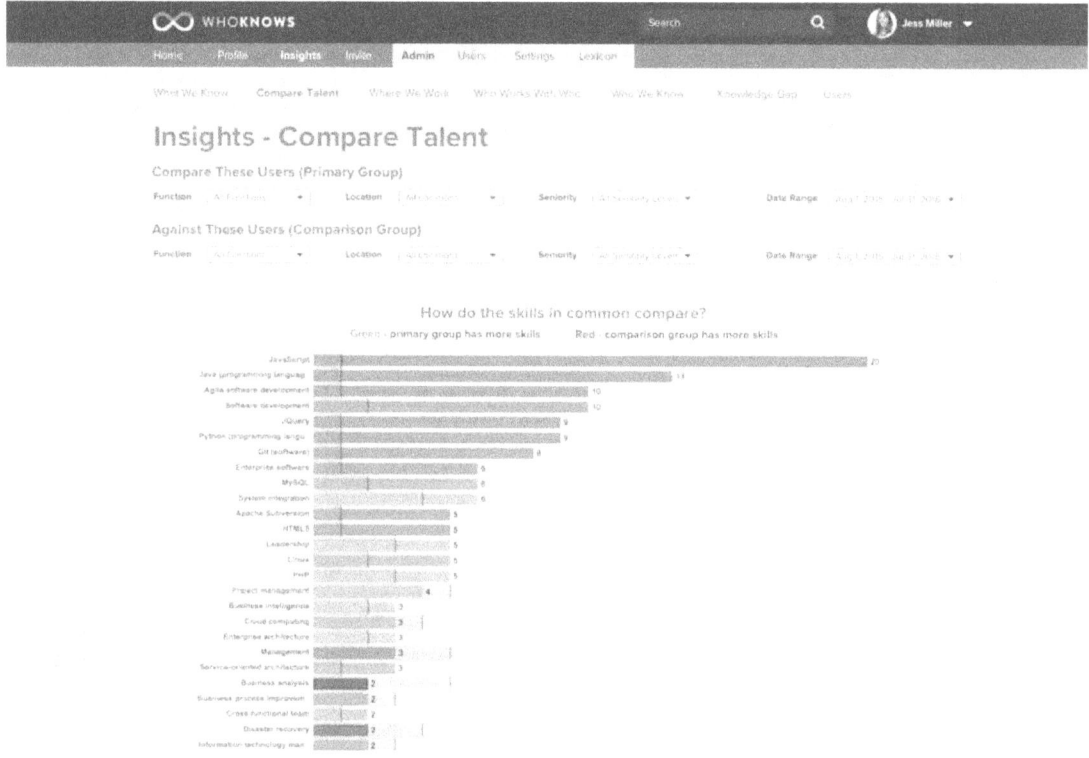

Here's what the insights dashboard offers:
• Discover talent analytics at your fingertips to better understand skills and experience for more accurate and reliable workforce planning.

• Gain insights into knowledge gaps and upcoming trends in new skills for better staffing and training planning.

• Increase enterprise collaboration by understanding valuable communication data as well as how people are collaborating.

Lightcast

Lightcast[25] finds purpose in sharing the insights that build communities, educators, and companies.

Lightcast uses the world's most advanced data analytics to provide insights needed to build and develop people, institutions, and communities.
Analysis of workforce intelligence data, collecting millions of job postings and career profiles daily to provide near-realtime insight into a fast-changing labor market.

Researchers use the database of more than one billion job postings and career profiles to examine the future of work, mapping the ways technological change is reshaping jobs and what workers need to know to keep up.

Access professional profiles, traditional labor market information, job postings, and compensation data.

See average comp salary ranges:

Software and Web Developers, Programmers, and Testers in United States

Executive Summary

Average Postings Competition Over an Average Supply of Regional Talent

566,003
Matching Profiles
The United States is about average for people matching your search. The national average for an area this size is 566,003 matching profiles, while there are 566,003 here.

$124,848
Compensation
The cost for talent is about average in the United States. The national median salary for people matching your search is $124,848, while you'll pay $124,848 here.

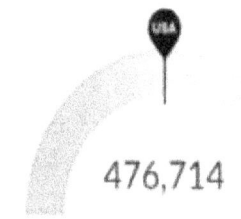
476,714
Postings Competition
Competition from online job postings is about average in the United States. The national average for an area this size is 476,714 job postings annually, while there are 476,714 here.

See Heat Map Trends for Specific Locations:

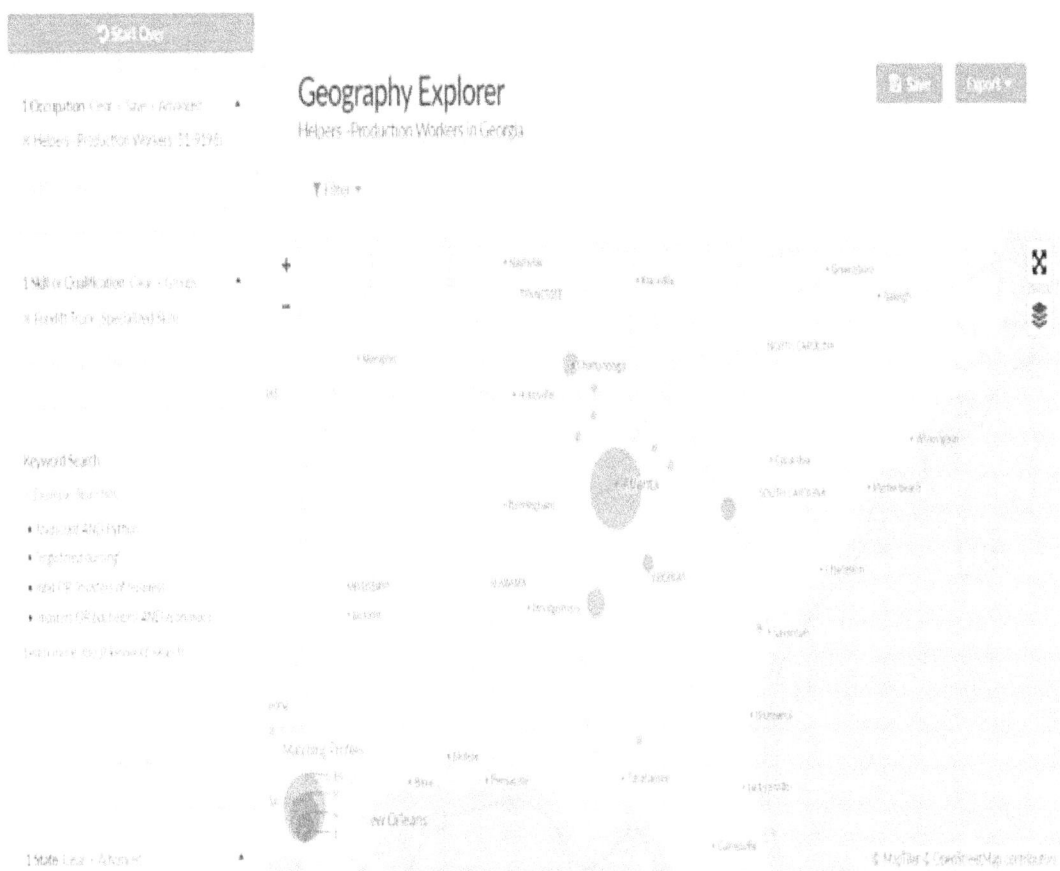

Monitor your competitors:

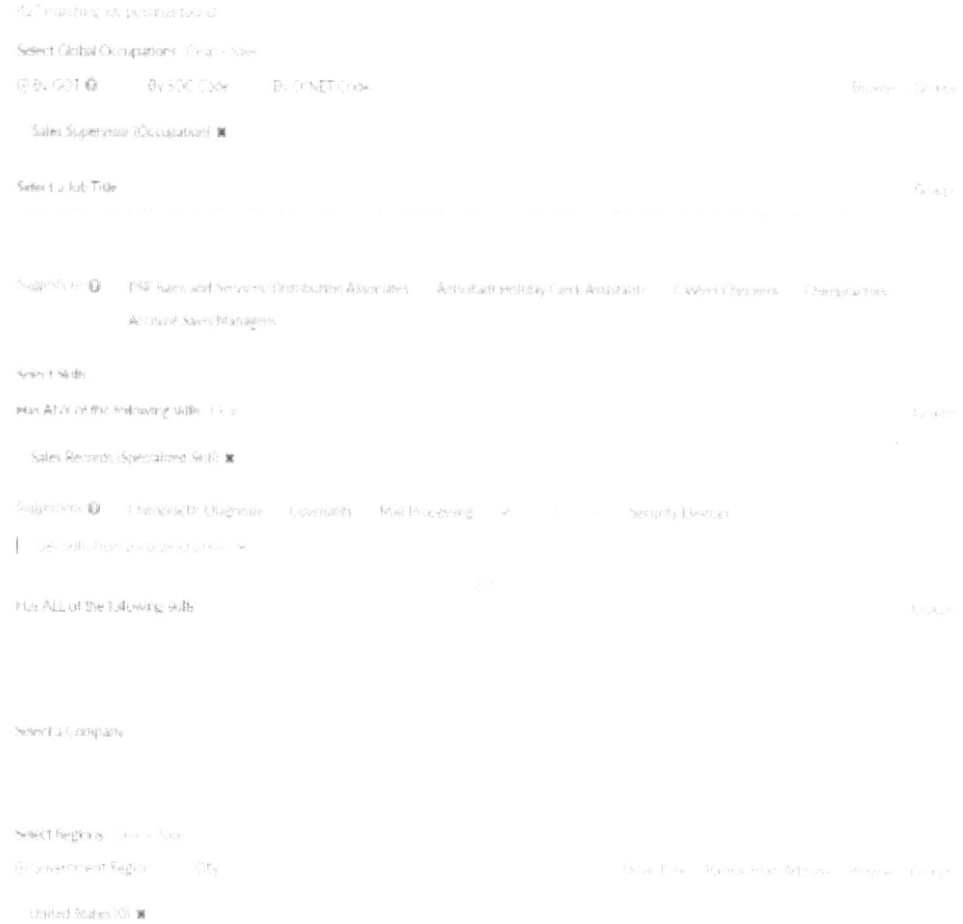

Here's what the data will answer:

- What are the best cities for a remote workforce?
- How are your competitors pursuing the candidates you need?
- What location should you focus recruiting efforts
- Quickly gain expertise in unfamiliar regions or talent market

• Where can you find the evidence, you need to challenge outdated strategies

Claro Analytics

Claro Analytics[26] is a data science platform that provides recruiters with insights into the people they've hired. Its services include predictive analytics, which help identify which candidates are most likely to quit; competitor comparison and ranking; and more.

Here's what the tool offers:
• Insights about current workforce metrics
• Competitive talent benchmarking
• Review Salary comp averages
• Helps identify passive job seekers

ZoomInfo 's Talent OS

ZoomInfo's Talent OS[27] is a software platform for recruiters and HR professionals. It provides access to a database of more than 133 million contacts, 100 million companies, and other crucial data.

ZoomInfo also offers recruitment features such as candidate matching and
automated emails.
Candidate and Company Intelligence: Discover passive talent using search filters to surface candidates ready for new opportunities. Search by company firmographics and view detailed organizational charts.

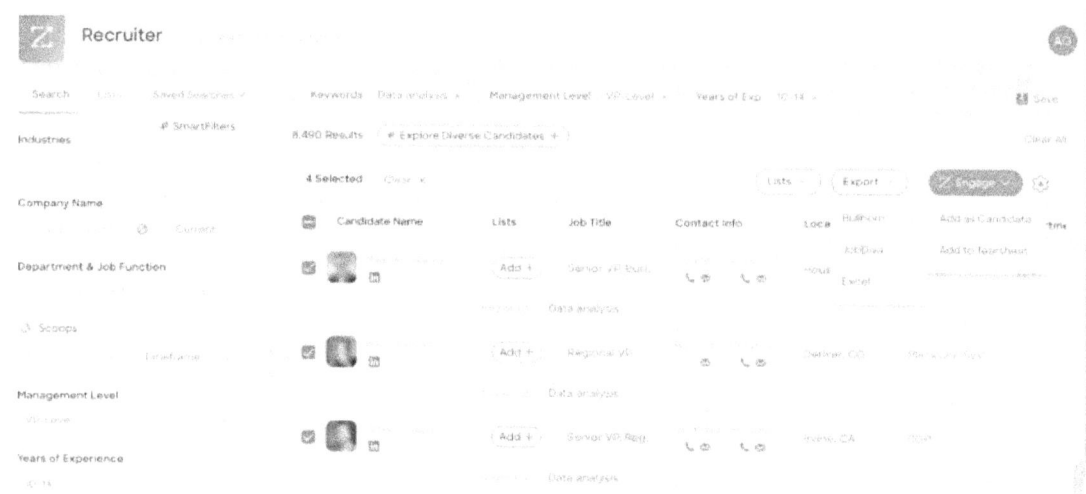

Comparably (Owned by Zoominfo) Comparably is a job placement service that provides employees with accurate and comprehensive data on wages and company culture, helping them to understand their true value and needs to make work better.

Browse Salaries
See what others are paid and compare your salary to see if you're underpaid. Salary data is contributed anonymously.
Browse States:

Salaries By City

Abilene, TX	Bangor, ME	Burlington, IA
Akron, OH	Baton Rouge, LA	Burlington, NC
Akutan, AK	Battle Creek, MI	Burlington, VT
Albany, GA	Bay City, MI	California, MD

Browse Companies:

Recent Salaries by Company

US Army Signal Corps	Cummins India	Sterling
Bayer Cropscience	GoDaddy	Total
Bowers & Wilkins	Federal	TNT
Clevertech	Cognizant Software	Lockton Companies
WebCare	AMERICAN SYSTEMS	BMC
Service Express	Essence	Finastra

Browse Company Data:

LinkedIn Talent Insights

LinkedIn Talent Insights[28] is a free tool for licensed users. It provides recruiters with data on the skills, work experience, and education of candidates. It also offers insights into hiring trends across industries, companies, and locations.

What makes LinkedIn Talent Insights unique?

• Real-time data including talent supply and demand, company reports, and employer branding metrics.
• Over 12 billion data points on talent, companies, jobs, skills, and schools from the world's largest professional network.

• 360-degree view of your organization, competitors, and the market.

• On-demand, simple talent intelligence tools with actionable insights, personalized

recommendations and learning resources.
You can start a new report and pull this data:

• Create a Talent Pool Report on various market details.
• Create a company report on your competitors.
• View your current company's report data.
The report includes:
• Who is employing talent in the region?
• What schools are producing this talent?
• What are related skills and titles for this talent?
• How is this talent engaging with your company on LinkedIn?

You can use this data to adjust your searches, focusing more on schools in the area, adding additional job tiles/skill sets, further optimize to your job descriptions, and adding more competitors to your search list.

Know where your company is losing talent to:

From what companies is Amazon winning and losing talent?

This module summarizes the companies from which Amazon has hired and lost talent from over the past 12 months.

Company (100)	Departures	Hires	Ratio	Net change
Amazon Web Services (AWS)	40	23		
Google	45	3	15	-42
Meta	35	3		
Microsoft	23	14	1.6	-9
Coinbase	10	6		
Apple	12	3	4	-9
SAP	0	14	+14	+14
Morgan Stanley	0	14	+14	+14
Canada Revenue Agency - Agence du revenu du Canada	0	12	+12	+12
University of Toronto	0	11	+11	+11

It is important to figure out where your employees are leaving to because it can provide valuable insights into why they are leaving and what you can do to prevent future turnover.

When employees leave, they take with them valuable knowledge, skills, and experience that can be difficult to replace. High turnover can also have a negative impact on team morale and productivity. Therefore, it is essential to identify the reasons why employees are leaving so that you can take steps to address these issues and improve retention.

Knowing where employees are leaving to can help you understand if they are leaving for better opportunities, higher pay, better benefits, or other reasons. For example, if you find that your employees are leaving to join competitors, it could be an indication that your competitors are offering better salaries, benefits, or career growth opportunities. This information can help you adjust your compensation and benefits packages, create better career development programs, or improve your company culture to retain your top talent.

LinkedIn Skills Graph

At the heart of our Skills Graph lies our skills taxonomy. The taxonomy is a curated list of unique skills and their intertwined relationships, each with detailed
information about those skills. It's built on a deep understanding of how skills power professional journeys, including what skills are required in a job, what skills a member has, and how members move from one position to the next.

The taxonomy is a frame work of structured skills that a professional need to function in that specific industry for example:

• If a member knows about Artificial Neural Networks, the member knows something about Deep Learning, which means the member knows something about Machine Learning.

• If a job requires Supply Chain
Engineering, having a skill in Supply Chain Management or Industry Engineering is definitely also relevant.

" To do this, our machine learning and artificial intelligence combs through massive amounts of data and suggests new skills and relations between them. As our Skills Graph continues to grow and learn with AI, we are committed to maintaining the high quality of the data and connections found in our taxonomy." – LinkedIn.com

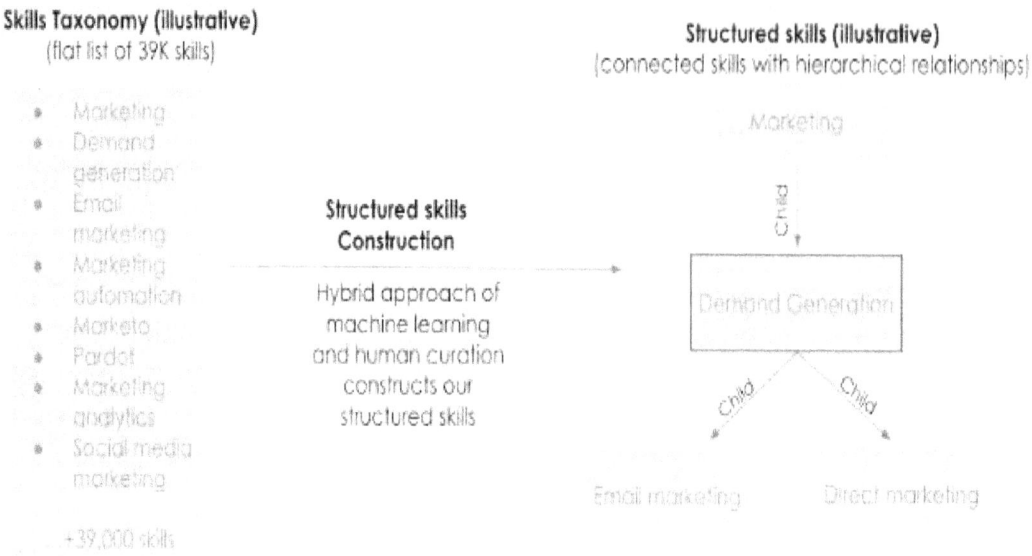

Structured skills consists of meaningful relationships between skills that empower deep reasoning to match members to relevant content such as jobs, learning material, and feed posts

(Source: LinkedIn.com)
Here's how to leverage this AI tool when publishing a job opening:

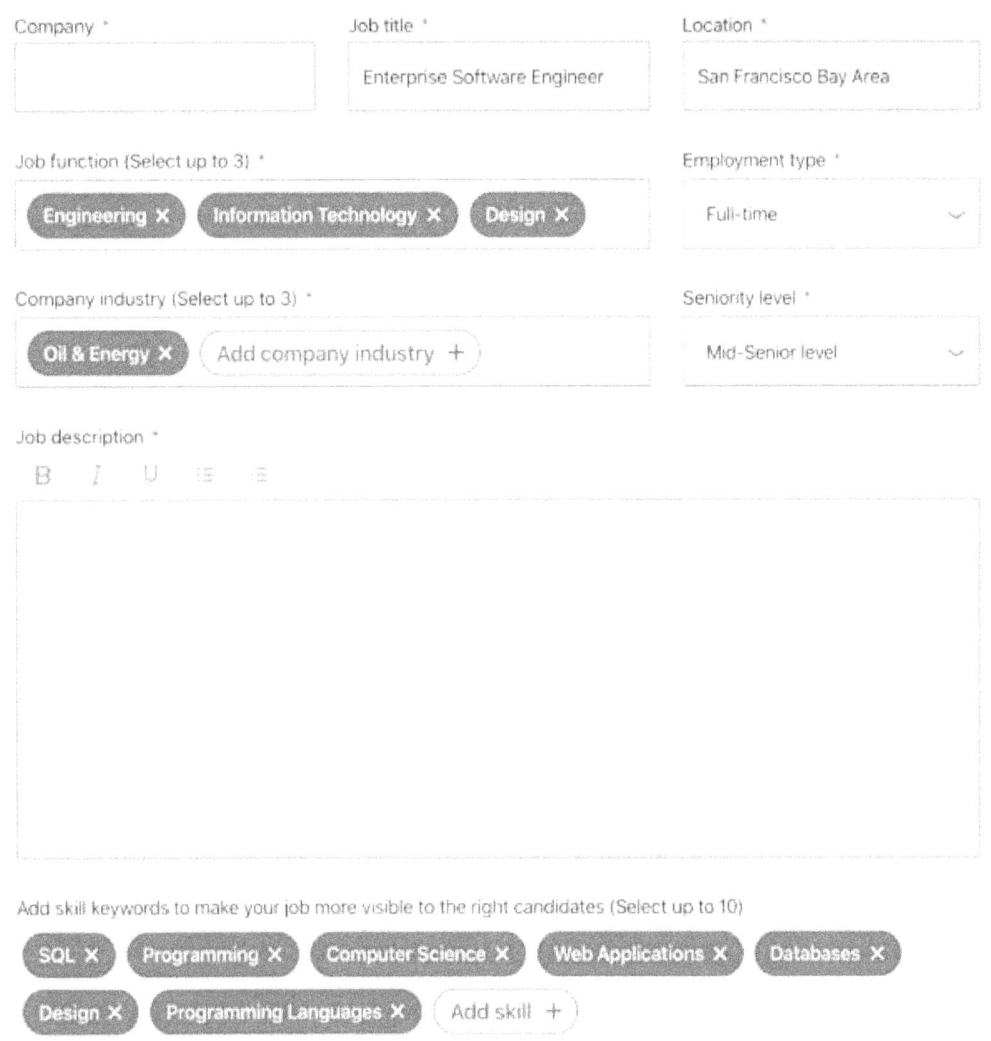

When hirers create a job post on the LinkedIn platform, we use machine learning and Structured skills to suggest explicit skills that we can tag the post with to increase discoverability

(Source: LinkedIn.com)

Bonus: LinkedIn Jobs

Try using this Boolean string to find salary comps posted on public job descriptions. site:www.linkedin.com/jobs salary|compensation "$50000..$150000" | "$50..$150" intitle:sourcer -intitle:jobs

In this example, I'm searching for Talent Sourcer jobs that include this salary range.

CareerBuilder's
Supply and Demand Portal

The Supply & Demand, as part of the Resume Database or Talent Discovery, delivers recruitment analytics and insights into active job seekers as well as your competitors to help you recruit and source more intelligently in today's marketplace.

Utilizing both of these workforce data points can give you a clear picture of how easy or hard it will be to attract top talent across certain industries, geographies and experience levels.

Features include

Keyword Search: search by keyword, job title or skill on a city, metro area, state or national level.
Compensation Data: see how your offered compensation compares to the
marketplace.

Heat Maps: see where jobs are posted versus where candidates are located • Top Job Posters: identify the companies that are competing for your talent.

Demographic Data: review demographic data of available candidates like years of experience to set better expectations.

Hiring Indicator: see how easy or difficult it will be to source your positions based on marketplace trends.

Custom Reporting: export your findings to PDF or Excel and have saved search results emailed to you.

Staffing Industry-Exclusive Tools: leverage data to generate sales leads and consult clients with labor market trends.

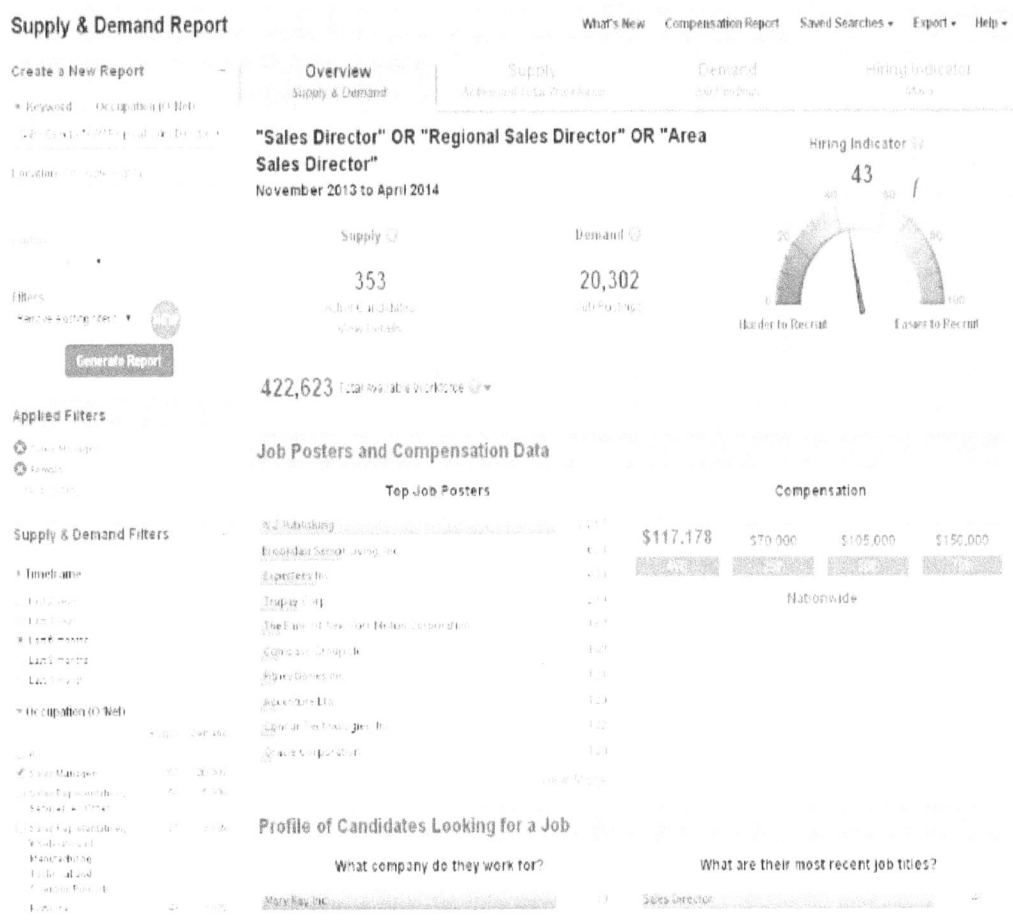

Talent Sourcing Resources

Eightfold.ai

Eightfold.ai[29] is a data platform for recruiters that helps them find their candidates faster. It does this by providing information on skills, experience, and education, as well as other relevant details needed for each role in an organization.

Here's the dashboard search section:

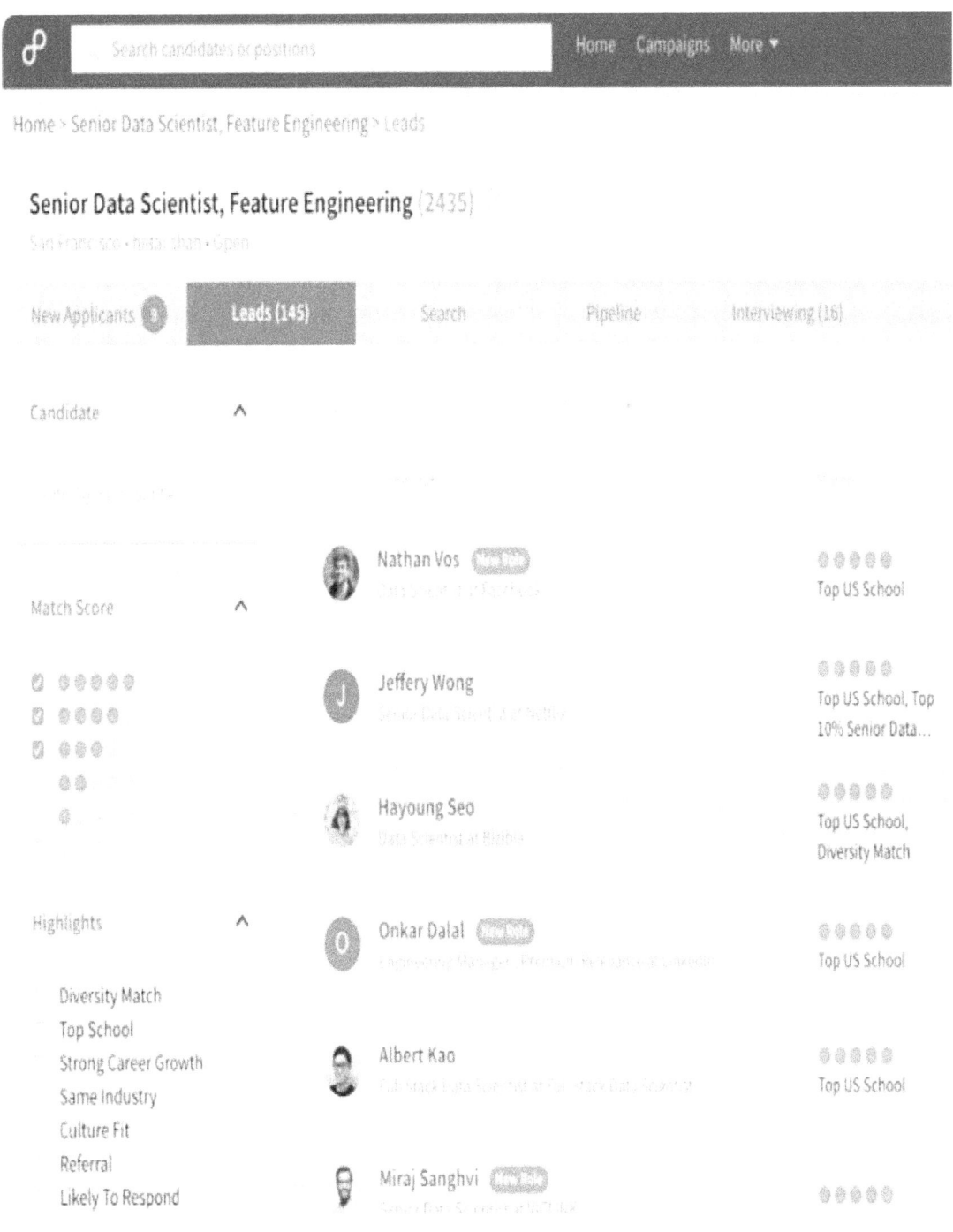

SeekOut

SeekOut[30] gives access to thousands of highly qualified leads (both internal and external) through its database. The platform has been designed to allow recruiters to search by keyword and location, making it very easy for you to filter out your results and focus on what matters most: finding the perfect candidates for your open jobs.

Analyze and understand key talent pools flexibly with powerful filters and interactive visualizations. View aggregate data on the locations, diversity, employment history, job titles, skills, and more of the candidates in your talent pool, and share insights with peers, hiring managers, and leadership.

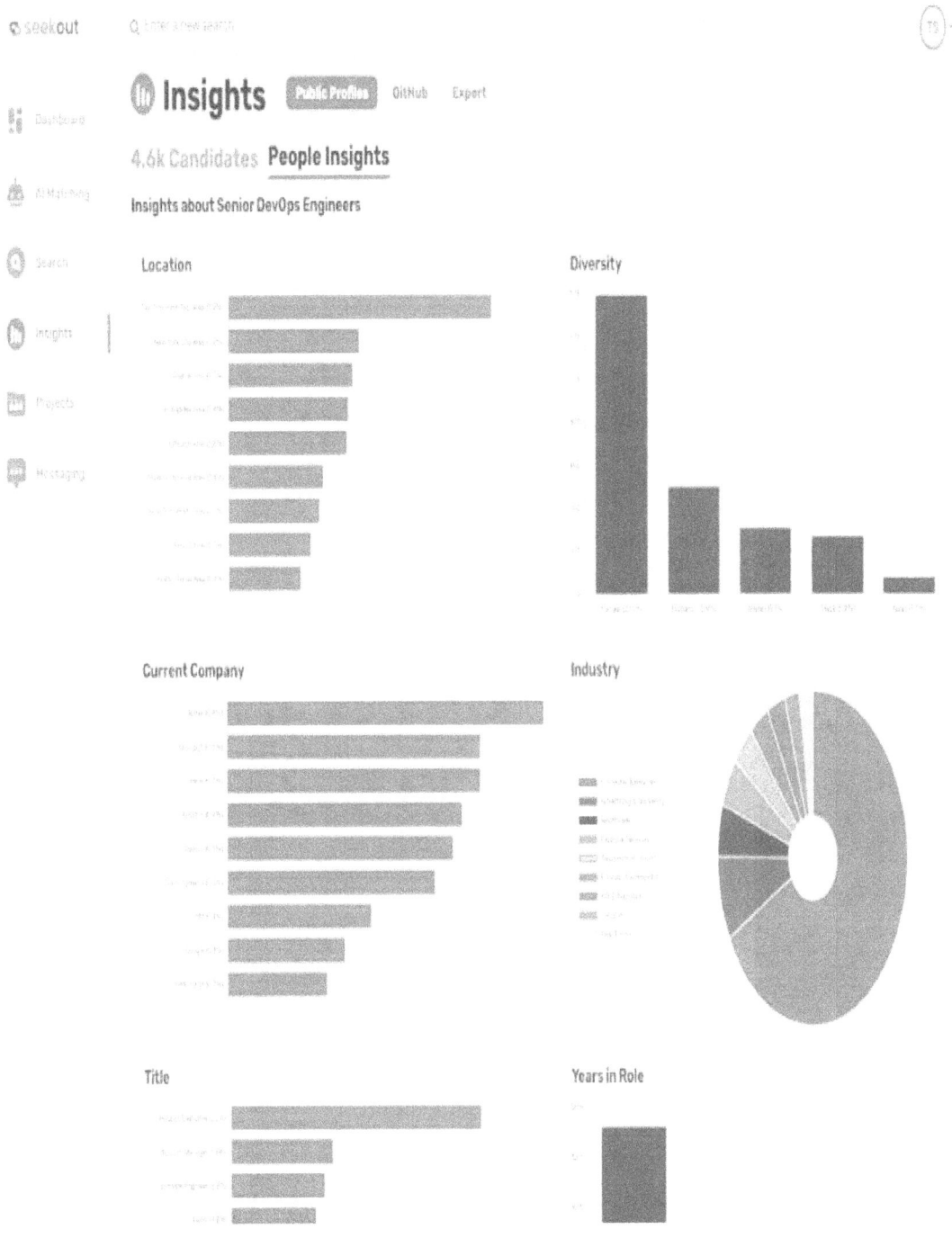

Search specific locations:

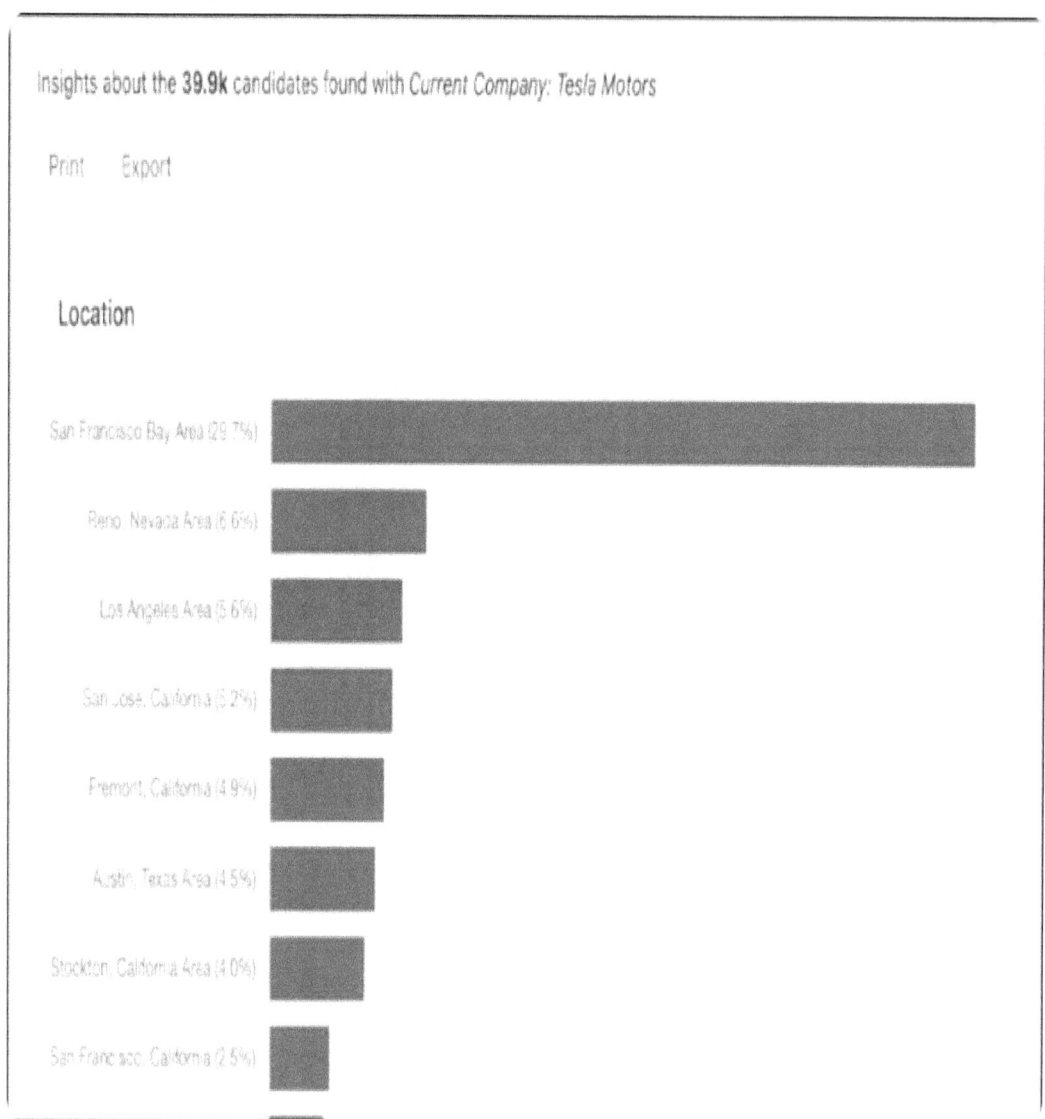

HireEZ (Hiretual)

Recruiters use hireEZ[31] to find job seekers, as well as to research companies,
employees, and competitors. The profiles on this site are

exceptionally thorough—they'll tell you everything from how many employees work at a company (and what their titles are) to what languages a candidate can speak fluently. If there's something specific, you're looking for in an employee profile, chances are good that it'll pop up here!

Its insights feature is particularly helpful for building a talent map, as it grants access to talent inflow and outflow data, competitive analytics, and diversity analysis.

To observe if there are any shifts in the job market, check out the percentage and number of candidates who have changed their jobs on the right side.

Search Job Titles:

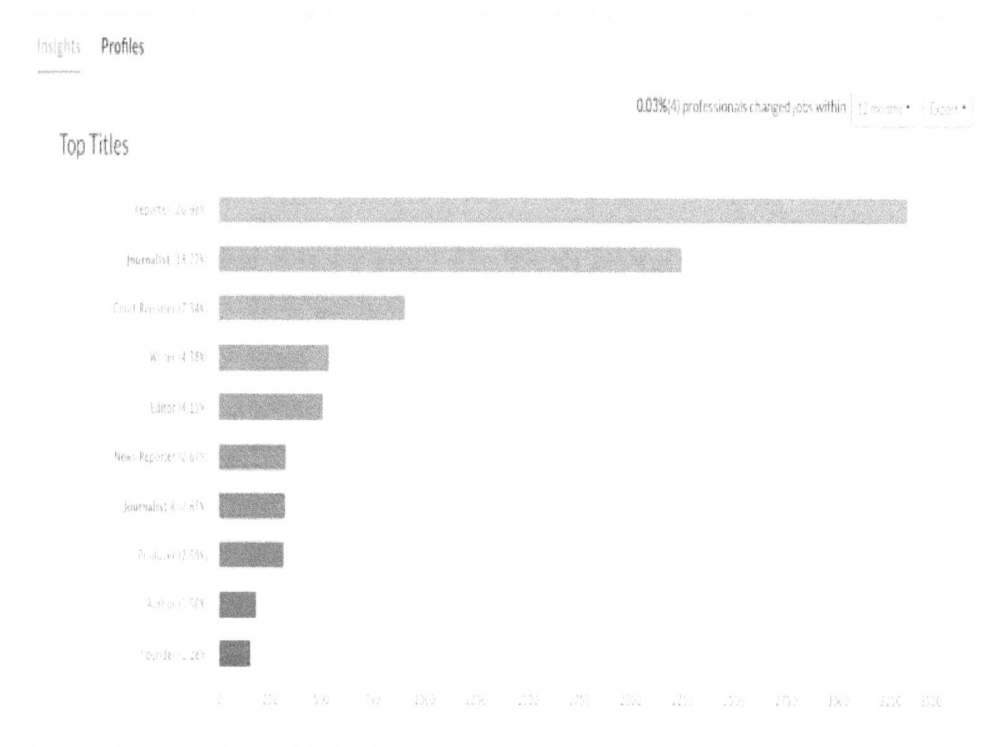

Mandatory or Preferred Skills:

Top Skills

Current or Past Companies:

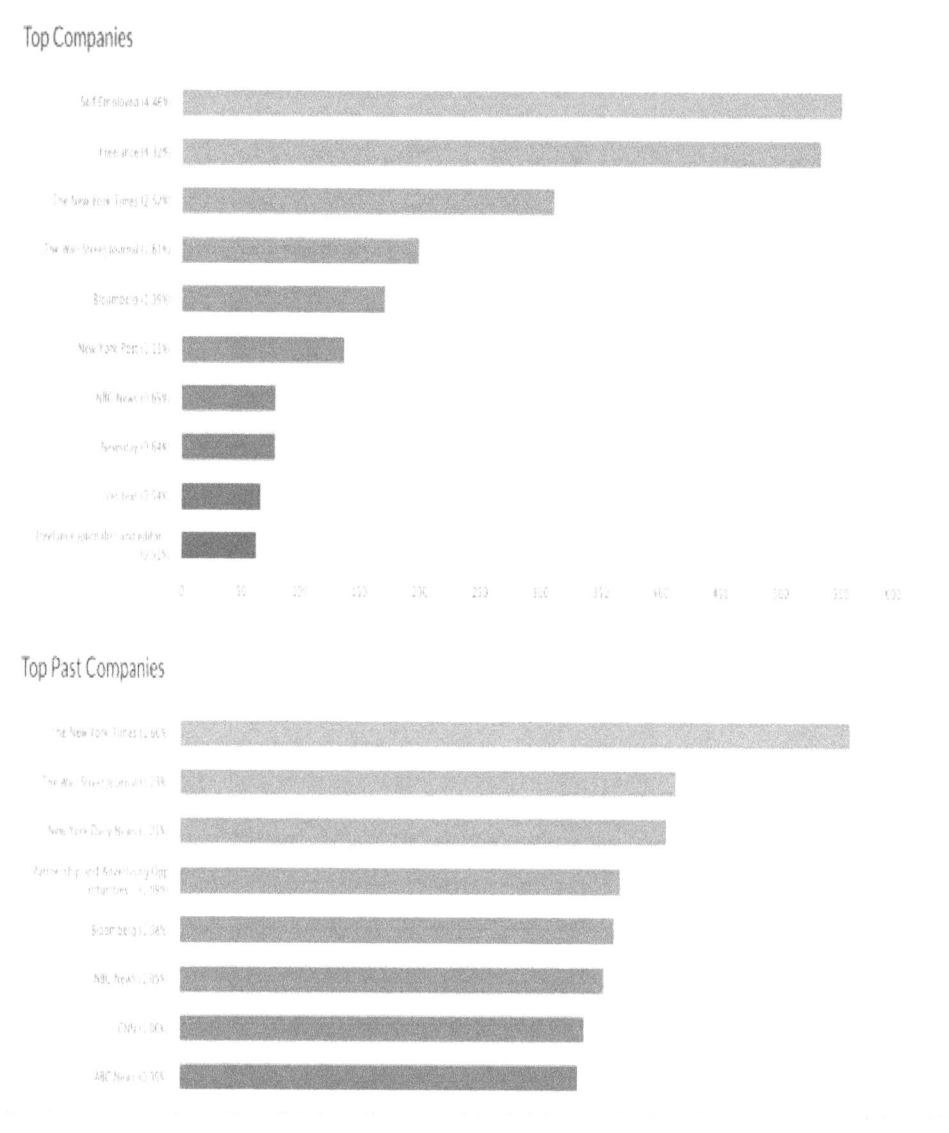

Industry Specific Intel:

Entelo

Entelo[32] is a recruiting data platform that provides candidate sourcing tools for recruiters. Its Candidate Insights feature is designed to help you find talent, build relationships with them, and ultimately hire them.

Here's what the tool offers:
• Robust Talent Pool Insights
• See How Candidates Stack Up
• Company Fit Score
• Company Insights

People Data Labs

People Data Labs[33] is a cloud-based recruiting tool that lets users filter
candidates by hundreds of data points, including their current location, education, job history, and social media activity. This data can be used to help recruiters quickly identify the best fit for an open position within their company or organization.

This tool allows you to access company search API data:
• Pre-calculated summaries of the people at over 18+ million companies

• Month-by-month employee headcount, including the count of gross additions and departures

• Breakdowns of employees by location, role, and seniority

• Ability to search and filter by
employee growth rates and churn rates within the Company Search API ***

Data is a powerful tool, and when used correctly, it can be an effective way to find the best candidates for your open positions. The tools listed in this chapter will allow you to access recruitment insight from a variety of sources, helping you make more informed decisions throughout the recruiting process.

Chapter 4: Implementing Research into a Talent Sourcing Strategy

When it comes to finding the best talent for your organization, there's a fine line between being thorough and being overly obsessive. You want to find the best candidates, but you also want to avoid wasting time on candidates that don't fit with your company's needs.

Fortunately, you now know that talent mapping can help you cut through the filler in half the time using data-driven decisions and market research. Now, here are some of the ways you can implement this
information into your talent sourcing strategy.

1. Use your market intelligence and analytics to define the job functions and skills needed for each role in your company

The data you've acquired should reveal the gaps that are currently preventing your company from achieving its strategic objectives. As such, you can use this information to inform your recruiting strategy by creating a detailed job description for each position. Ask yourself questions like:

• What are the skills required to
perform this role?
• In what ways does the candidate's background need to reflect this skill set?
• What is the ideal career path for someone in this position?
• What does a candidate in this position expect to gain from the role?

2. Personalize, perfect, and experiment with your outreach messages

Once you have determined who your target candidates are, it is time to start writing outreach messages. You should use a template that can be personalized and customized for each candidate. Remember that the goal of an outreach message is to get the attention of your target candidate and make them interested in learning more about your opportunity. As such, it's important to write with personality and keep it short, simple, and clear—don't waste time on lengthy introductions or unnecessary details about what you do (this will come later).

Fortunately, you now have ample insight and data-backed reasoning that you can use to convey why this role matters so much for both sides: What value does this person add? How will they benefit from joining the team? How will the team benefit from having them join?

3. Modify and expand your search terms to discover "hidden-gem" candidates

Chances are, there are dozens of recruiters out there who are searching for and contacting the same exact candidates you're targeting. So, instead of focusing on keywords and job titles that are common among all recruiters, try modifying your search terms to include more specific qualifications and experience that only represent a small subset of candidates (e.g., "JavaScript developer" instead of just "developer").

This is particularly helpful for roles that may have different names across separate companies. You might use one of the tools mentioned in the previous chapter to list

these titles and ensure you have every base covered as you source.

4. Complete progress reports and check-ins to maintain your existing talent

As your talent sourcing efforts mature, it's important to keep an eye on how things are going by regularly checking in with your existing employees.

There are two main reasons for this: First, check-ins can be used to identify and address problems before they can cause a rift between you and your employees. Second, check-ins can also be used as an opportunity to update job descriptions based on their feedback, keep employees motivated and excited about their work, or even just provide some encouragement when needed!

5. Continue dedicating ample time for your talent mapping efforts

As we've discussed, the time and effort spent on a talent map will determine the quality of your supply chain. To that end, we recommend dedicating ample time for your talent mapping efforts. It's important to stay on top of the latest trends in your industry and make changes as necessary so that you can provide a consistent experience for candidates throughout their journey.

***

While the talent sourcing process is highly complex and requires significant resources, it can also be incredibly rewarding— especially when backed by data. If done well, your company will benefit from a more diverse workforce that helps fill key roles with the right candidates. In addition, you will have a better understanding of how to work with these new employees once they join your team!

How to present data to hiring managers or recruiting managers

Hiring managers and recruiting managers are busy people. They have a lot on their plates and often need to make quick decisions about candidates.

You're probably dealing with many other candidates as well, so it's important that you communicate clearly and quickly throughout your working relationship. The best way to do so? Using data.

Here's how.

1. Decide on communication preferences and frequency early on

Deciding what information, you should share and how often is important. To start, determine the amount of time you have to work with them before they make a decision (this is usually a few weeks). Then, consider what kind of information they need to know in order to make that decision. For example:

• **How frequently do they want updates?** If this is an internal hire and there are only two people who need to review resumes, then weekly or monthly updates may be fine. But if it's an external hire and there are multiple stakeholders involved, then daily or even hourly updates might be more helpful.

• **How detailed does each update need to be?** The hiring manager probably doesn't want every single detail about your conversation with a candidate (who did not receive any offer) included in every single email unless they ask for it specifically. Equally, you want to make sure you never leave anything important out.

2. Keep recruitment expectations realistic with data-backed reasoning

Data is a great way to help hiring managers and recruiting managers understand where the company is right now: Its objective helps keep expectations realistic by providing a "hard number" that makes it easier to calculate the future of the
organization.

To present this information, you can use tables or lists, which are more digestible than paragraphs of text. This will also save time for busy hiring managers who don't have much time on their hands.

3. Regularly let them know where you are, how you got there and where you're going

Depending on your communication agreements, it's a good idea to frequently update your hiring manager on your talent sourcing progress. Not only will this help you hold yourself accountable, but it'll also show the hiring manager that you're a proactive recruiter who takes initiative to get things done.
In most cases, these don't need to be particularly extensive. You could update them on:

- The number of candidates you've contacted
- The status of each candidate's application (i.e., whether they've completed the application, submitted an updated resume, etc.)
- What method you used to
communicate with each candidate (phone call vs. email vs. LinkedIn message)

4. Create reports and include visuals to objectively rank your candidates

When it's time to present data to the hiring manager, don't just send them a
spreadsheet. Instead, consider creating reports that include visualizations and graphics. Here's why:

• **Reports allow you to objectively rank candidates based on specific parameters:** For example, if your client wants to hire someone with experience in Excel but isn't sure which candidates have used it in the past, use graphs and charts that show how much each candidate uses Excel per hour of work over the course of their career. This way, they can make decisions based on objective data instead of hunches or assumptions based on interviews alone.

• **Reports make complex information more digestible for hiring managers:** When you create reports that include visualizations, it's easier for hiring managers to make sense of large amounts of data. In fact, studies have shown that people are better able to understand and retain information when they see it presented in charts, graphs and other visual

representations (Sage Journal).

5. Maintain credibility and trust throughout the relationship

By maintaining these practices, you will be able to establish a positive relationship based on hard data and informed reasoning. Still, your work doesn't stop as soon as specifics are agreed on. You still need to uphold these principles well into the future. So, be sure you:

• **Keep your manager informed of any changes in the data or their
interpretation:** If you discover that there's a discrepancy between what you reported on and what the hard data actually signifies, let

them know immediately so they can make an accurately informed decision.
• **Maintain a high level of integrity:** It's no secret that data analysis can be subject to human error, so make sure that your intentions are always honest when working with hiring managers.
• **Make sure you're always striving to do better:** Don't take the easy way out and stop at the first set of data that seems to support your argument. Keep digging until you find

something more concrete —or at least until you're certain that what you have is correct.

Putting it all together

I recommend demoing and reviewing the talent mapping tools and resources that we discussed within the book. After your team has selected the appropriate tools, the next step will be to pull and compile relevant data (you can present your findings in Excel, a PDF, or with a PowerPoint).
Finally, meet with your recruiting manager or hiring manager to discuss a talent sourcing strategy.

Once you have the data, use it when creating search strings and targeting demographic information. Make sure to tag or record your efforts within your ATS or CRM systems, as this will help your employer gain access to data mapping licenses in the future and increase their return on investment.

Chapter 5: Presenting your Talent Map

By incorporating your talent mapping research into your intake meetings and team meetings can be an effective way to build trust with your hiring team and demonstrate your value as a recruiter. By regularly sharing your labor market intelligence and recruiting metrics, you can help your hiring managers make informed decisions about their hiring needs and stay up-to-date on the latest trends and best practices in talent acquisition.

During intake meetings, you can use your talent mapping research to help define the ideal candidate profile for each role and provide insights into the current labor market conditions. This can help you set realistic expectations with your hiring managers and develop a targeted
recruitment strategy that aligns with their goals and objectives.
In bi-weekly team meetings, you can provide updates on your recruiting activities and share your progress toward meeting your hiring goals. You can also share any challenges or roadblocks you have
encountered and solicit feedback and ideas from your team members to help overcome them.

By consistently showcasing your talent mapping research and recruiting metrics, you can build a case for the value you bring to the organization and establish yourself as a trusted partner and advisor to your hiring team. Over time, this can help you build long-term relationships with your hiring managers, increase their confidence in your abilities, and ultimately improve your effectiveness as a recruiter.

Here's an example of how you can influence a hiring manager:

Say company X is looking for a software manager with 10 years' experience in the eCommerce industry. You provide comparative data and explain that the salary they are willing to offer is 20 percent less than the industry average. You can also include that job titles tend to be titled Director and above with the data that you've pulled. By presenting your talent map you will be able to persuade decision makers.

Using Talent Maps to influence decisions

By simply creating a talent map, you are using data evidence to prove your points. This will help establish your credibility with your hiring manager and set realistic deliverable expectations on each individual job requisition. I recommend coming prepared to the intake meeting with a talent mapping example. You can further expand after you've completed the initial meeting.

Here's how a talent map can improve your relationship with your leadership team:

1. Demonstrate knowledge
2. Shows good judgment
3. Being persistent builds trust
4. Humbles the Hiring Manager
5. Helps drive strategy

Building a Talent Map into the process

Have your recruiting manager pull job requisition data from the past. Then have your team create specific talent maps per niche area. Building a future plan will help alleviate problems in the future and help build a talent pipeline.

Prep before an Intake Meeting:

1. Develop your communication strategy:
• Pre-intake email sent to leader
• Agenda planning and further prep

2. Research the role(s)

• Pull recent hire data from ATS for benchmarking
• Research past hires – include retention & long-term successes

- Collaborate with peer recruiters (cross team collaboration)

3. Research the hiring manager and broader team ORG structure

4. Research the business and understand your competition

- During the intake present your talent mapping and recruiting funnel metrics

5. Build rapport quickly

- During the intake meeting allow time to learn about their leadership style and

team dynamics
- Use a template intake form to provide meaningful consistent discussion.
- Ensure full understanding of the role and the priorities of the team.

6. Bi-weekly Meetings

- Send a follow up about next steps after the meeting
- Use the bi-weekly meet to present further talent mapping data
- Showcase your talent pipeline
- Discuss the candidate slate
- Systematically map your target list and document progress
- Leverage talent mapping tools o Internal ATS systems
  o External Tools

Staying organized with help:
- Leverage this data in the future
- Showcase your ROI

Example of a Talent Map that I presented to one of my hiring managers:

Slate of Candidates for the HM to review:

Channel Sales Director					RECRUITER ACTION REQUIRED CHECK BOX IF STEP HAS BEEN COMPLETED			
	LinkedIn	Other	Other	Source	Contacted	Screened	Interviewed	Hired
New York, NY	www.linkedir	https://twitte	https://plus	LinkedIn				
	http://www.l	https://twitte	X	LinkedIn				
	http://www.l	https://twitte	X	LinkedIn				
	http://www.l	X	X	LinkedIn				
Framingham, MA	http://www.l	X	X	LinkedIn				
	https://www	https://www	X	Talentbin				
Ewing, NJ	https://www	http://www.r	X	Talentbin				
	www.linkedir	https://twitte	http://www	LinkedIn				
	https://www	https://www	http://www	Talentbin				
Herndon, VA	https://www	https://twitte	X	Talentbin				
	https://www	https://twitte	X	Talentbin				
Atlanta, GA	https://www	https://twitte	https://www	Talentbin				
	https://www	https://twitte	https://plus	Talentbin				
Charlotte, NC	https://www	https://twitte	http://www	Talentbin				
	https://www	X	X	LinkedIn				
Plano, TX	https://www	https://twitte	https://plus	Talentbin				
	https://www	https://twitte	X	Talentbin				
Chicago/ Lisle	https://www	https://www	https://twit	Talentbin				
	https://www	https://twitte	X	Talentbin				

Create a progress report to showcase updates on candidates in your pipeline: Note: After the initial intake meeting has been completed. I recommend using your bi-weekly meetings to focus more on talent mapping updates. Share your candidate slate and come prepared with recruiting metric funnel data etc.

Boolean string examples:

Channel Sales Director

New York, NY

Linkedin String	https://www.linkedin.com/vsearch/o?keywords=%22Channel%20Sales%22%20AND%20%22B2B%2
Indeed String	("Channel Sales") anytitle:("Channel Sales Manager" OR "Sales Manager" OR "Sales Director" OR "D
Google String	(intitle:resume | inurl:resume) -job -sample -eoe -submit -free -template (New York, NY) ("Channel S
Bing String	(intitle:resume | inurl:resume) -job -sample -eoe -submit -free -template (New York, NY) ("Channel
Facebook String	https://www.facebook.com/search/145282138923975/job/108424279189115/employer-location/
Google Plus String	site:plus.google.com (lives * New York, NY) ("Channel Sales Manager" | "Sales Manager" | "Sales Dire
Twitter String	https://twitter.com/search?q=%22Channel-Sales-Manager%22+-job+-jobs+-eoe+lang%3Aen+near

Social media communities to target:

site:linkedin.com "Title of group logo" -intitle:profiles -inurl:dir -inurl:jobs

Channel Sales Director

Software Sales Careers
Enterprise Software Sales Professionals
IBM Software Sales Opportunities
Technical Sales Group (software/data/internet/wireless)
Software Sales Professionals
Software Industry: Sales & Marketing Executives (ex-IBM, Oracle, SAP, i2, EMC, BMC, Siebel, ETC)
Software Sales & Marketing People
Software Development Jobs - Powered by IvyExec.com
Enterprise Software Sales Engineering
IT & Software and Services Sales Professionals
IT/Software Business Development,Sales,Marketing,Outsourcing and Offshoring
http://www.meetup.com/Triangle-Assasin/
http://www.meetup.com/San-Francisco-Software-Sales-Directors-and-VPs/members/65028502/

Recent PR news:

Latest News and Press Releases

CA Technologies Named Market Leader in APM by Independent Analyst Firm

CA Technologies to lay off an additional 600 workers

CA, INC. Files SEC form 8-K, Costs Associated with Exit or Disposal Activities, Regulation FD Disclosure

Embarcadero to Acquire CA Technologies Data Modeling Business

CA Technologies Partners with the Wharton School's Mack Institute for Innovation Management

Emulex appoints former CA Technologies exec as VP of sales

CA Technologies Awards Scholarships to the Next Generation of Mainframe Leaders

Technology Strategy Not Just an IT Responsibility, Global Study Reveals

Finding application problems before they impact users

NASDAQ Decliners Watch List: Mylan, Inc. (NASDAQ:MYL) and CA Technologies (NASDAQ:CA) Added to Growing Stock Report's NASDAQ Decliners Watch List.

CA Tech appoints APAC head

CA Technologies appoints Kenneth Arredondo as president & general manager of Asia Pacific

Citrix and CA Technologies to provide native integration of NetScaler and ...

CA Technologies launches MDM suite

MWC 2014 Video: Why Did CA Technologies Buy Layer 7?

CA Technologies- Feb 26, 5:30pm | New Offerings

CA Technologies- Feb 26, 4:00pm | New Offerings

RSA News: Citrix and CA Technologies Team Up

Talent Neuron location data:
Suggesting alternative places to source:

Alternate Location	Job Volume*	Candidate Supply	Posting Period	Hiring Scale
New York-Northern New Jersey-Long Island, NY	37	400	45 days	76
Chicago-Joliet-Naperville, IL	45	400	46 days	80
San Jose-Sunnyvale-Santa Clara, CA	32	300	44 days	71
Atlanta-Sandy Springs-Marietta, GA	20	200	42 days	76
Dallas-Fort Worth-Arlington, TX	27	200	42 days	81
Boston-Cambridge-Quincy, MA	23	200	45 days	89
San Francisco-Oakland-Fremont, CA	34	200	44 days	90
Washington-Arlington-Alexandria, DC	40	200	46 days	93
Phoenix-Mesa-Glendale, AZ	7	100	42 days	74
Charlotte-Gastonia-Rock Hill, NC	4	< 100	42 days	77
Tampa-St. Petersburg-Clearwater, FL	3	< 100	41 days	
Trenton-Ewing, NJ	1	< 100	42 days	

Demographic information:

Gender / Ethnicity (Nationwide)
Candidate Supply: 6,300

	Women		Men	
	2,250	Caucasian		2,930
	150	African-American		150
	125	Asian		175
	200	Hispanic		225
	45	Other		50
	Total: 2,770		Total: 3,530	

Educational Attainment (Nationwide)

Candidate Supply: 6,300 — Current Openings: 653

Supply	Level	Openings
625	High School	4
1,550	Associate's	2
3,045	Bachelor's	453
1,000	Master's	189
80	Doctorate	5

Competitor intel based on job openings:

Competitor Landscape

SAP	239
Revoyr & Associates	80
IBM	73
Microsoft	65
NCR Corporation	52
DELL	51
CommScope	51
E.I. DuPont De Nemours & Company	51
MarketStar	47
Emc Corporation	39
Siemens AG	35
Nigel Frank	35
VMware	35
FireEye, Inc.	34
Hewlett-Packard Company	33
ADP, Inc.	30
NetApp	24
Lenovo	24
Turning Technologies	23
Samsung	23
Sales Staff	22
Verizon	21
Apple Inc.	20
Technology Focused Venture Capital Firm	20
Leidos	20
CenturyLink	19
Interactive Intelligence, Inc.	18
Cisco	18

Locations posted in job postings:

Location Landscape

Location	
Chicago, IL	105
Atlanta, GA	90
New York, NY	86
Houston, TX	68
Boston, MA	65
San Francisco, CA	58
Los Angeles, CA	54
Dallas, TX	54
Denver, CO	51
Washington, DC	48
Phoenix, AZ	40
Austin, TX	39
Raleigh, NC	34
McLean, VA	34
Miami, FL	29
Minneapolis, MN	29
Seattle, WA	28
Reston, VA	26
Columbus, OH	26
Irvine, CA	26
San Jose, CA	24

CareerBuilder Supply & Demand report:

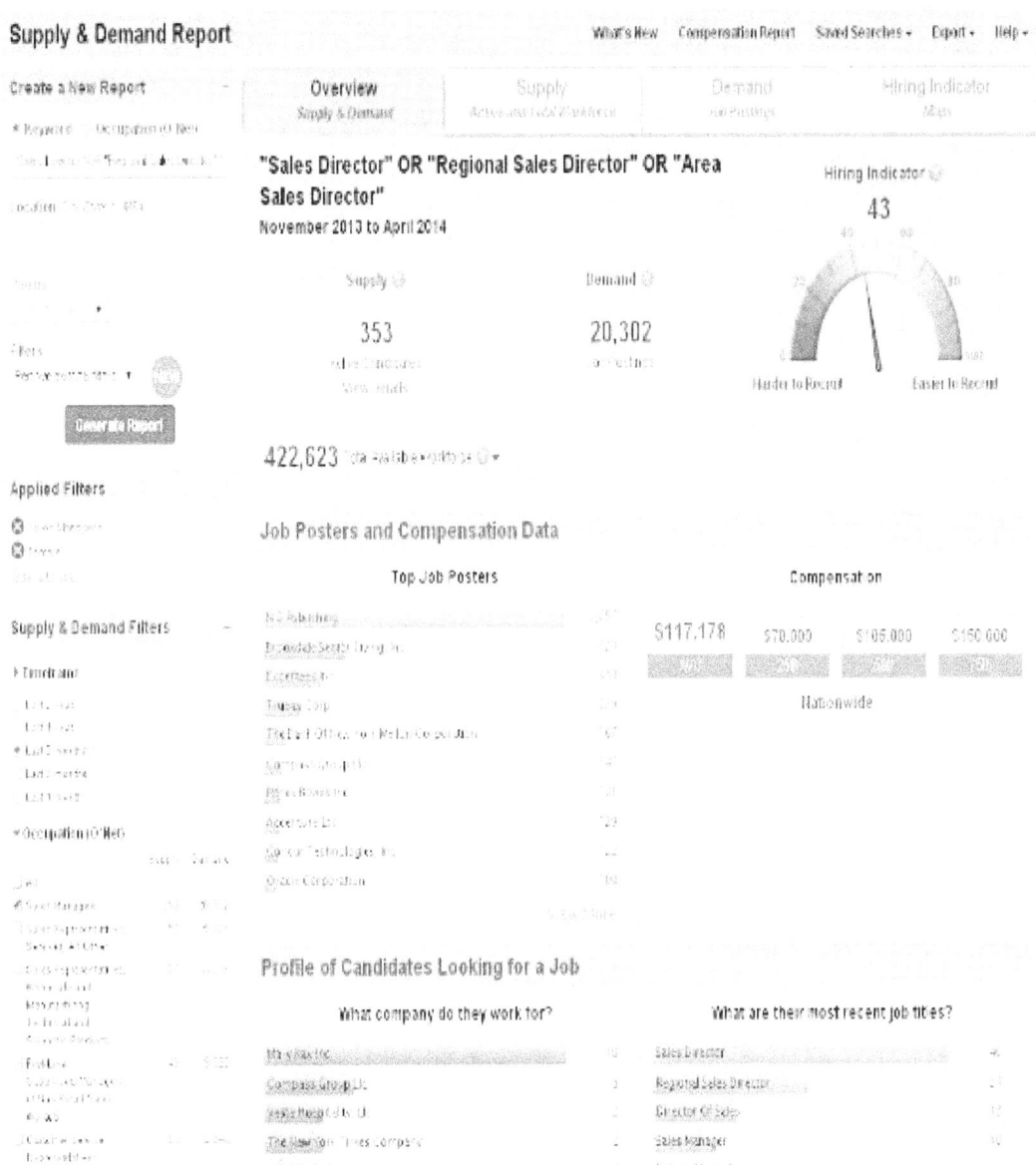

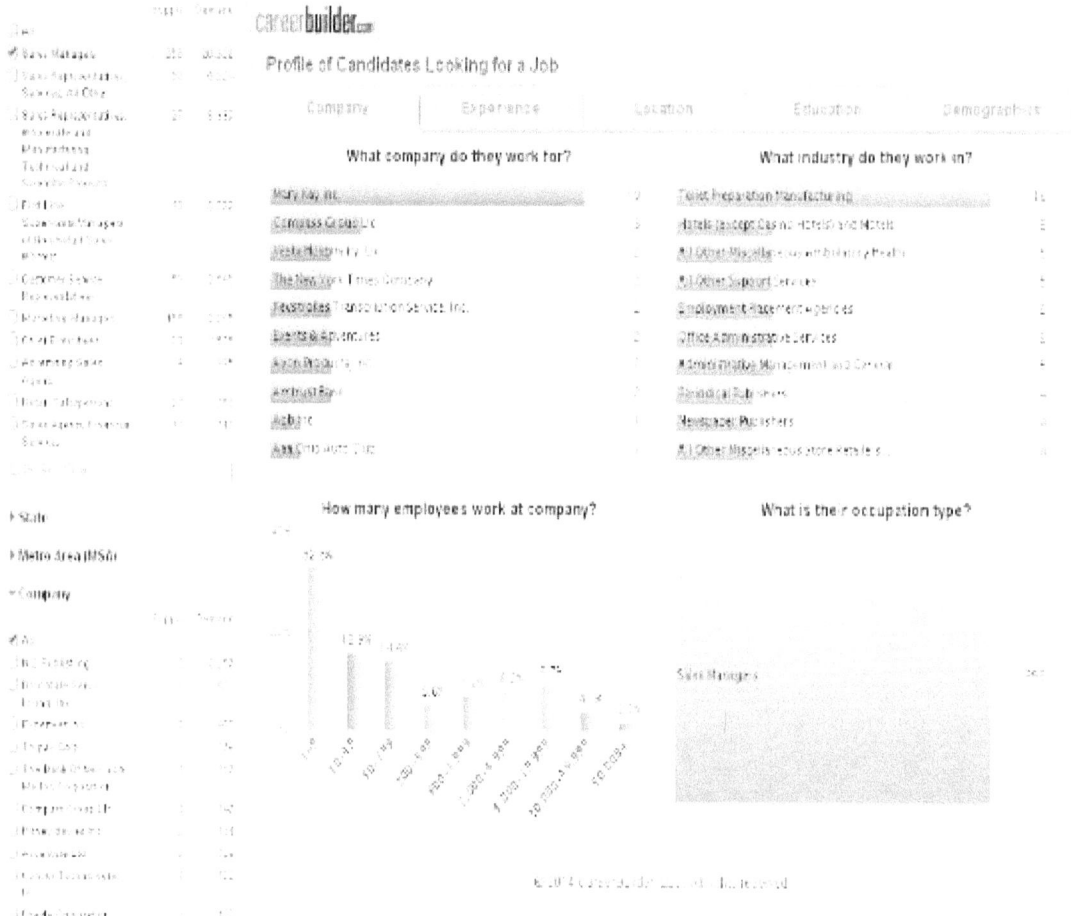

Top competitor's intel:

Future Predictions

Of course, it's hard to predict the future but by analyzing data trends we may have a window into what the next few years will bring into the recruitment industry. A recent post by *Miguel Mayorga* inspired me to add these predictions below.

One trend that I see is that economic and demographic challenges will continue to make it difficult for companies to invest and expand their hiring initiatives.

This means that employers will need to work harder to offer attractive options for candidates who place a high value on worklife balance. Companies will need to realize that remote work is here to stay.

In order to succeed in this environment, it's crucial for companies to shift their focus from degrees to skills when it comes to hiring. Less people are pursuing four-year bachelor degrees and instead going straight into the job market.

This means that talent acquisition and intelligence teams need to be efficient in processing data about skills, both internally and externally, in order to make informed decisions about potential hires in a competitive market.

Creating a talent mapping strategy will be vital for your team's success long term.
ChatGPT AI Tool

For years now there has been a prediction about how AI is going to take over recruiting. So far there have been some tools that have helped recruiters be more efficient and better, but most of the tools out there so far have not lived up to the hype.

In comes, Open AI's Chat GPT-3 which I know is not going to replace any recruiters at the moment, but it's the best AI tool that has been released to the public.

How can you use the tool for talent mapping?

Use AI tool to ask any question that you might want to know more research on. Using AI, it will instantly construct an answer using a variety of data resources online.?

Here's how to get started:

Once you create an account you can ask this AI tool virtually any type of question. So, I decided to ask several questions that would assist in creating a talent map:

Q: What's Amazon's main competitors?

A: Amazon is a large, diversified company that operates in many different industries, including e-commerce, cloud computing, and artificial intelligence. As such, it has many competitors in various sectors. Some of Amazon's main competitors in the ecommerce space in North America include eBay, Walmart, and Target. In the cloud computing space, Amazon's main competitors in North America include Microsoft Azure and Google Cloud. In the artificial intelligence space, Amazon's main competitors in North America include IBM Watson and Google Cloud AI.

Using this tool was been an eye-opening experience. I definitely recommend reviewing it further.

www.ingramcontent.com/pod-product-compliance
Lightning Source LLC
Chambersburg PA
CBHW082208220526
45470CB00010B/3094